HENRIETTA SZOLD AND YOUTH ALIYAH: FAMILY LETTERS, 1934-1944

Edited by
ALEXANDRA LEE LEVIN

HERZL PRESS
New York

HADASSAH
THE WOMEN'S ZIONIST
ORGANIZATION OF AMERICA, INC.

50 West 58th Street, New York, N.Y. 10019

Hadassah is pleased to share these letters written by Henrietta Szold, the Founder of Hadassah, to her family in Baltimore.

Written between 1934 and 1944, they offer a sensitive, in-depth presentation of events in Palestine during this difficult period and arouse renewed respect for the courage, vision, and steadfastness of the Yishuv.

Hadassah expresses its heartfelt appreciation to Alexandra Lee Levin, niece of Henrietta Szold, for her generous contribution of these family letters, which heretofore have never been available for publication, and for her warm biographical additions.

Appreciation is also due to Kalman Sultanik, Chairman of the Herzl Press, and to its Director of Publications, Sam E. Bloch, for helping make possible the publication of this book.

We believe all who read these letters will once again be inspired by the unusual gifts of leadership of Henrietta Szold and will cherish this volume as a special memento of Hadassah's 75th Anniversary Year.

Ruth Popkin, President

Charlotte Jacobson, Chairman
75th Anniversary Committee

CONTENTS

PREFACE

By Akiva Lewinsky

I feel very privileged to have been asked by Hadassah to write an Introduction to this book of Henrietta Szold's correspondence with her family during the first ten years of Youth Aliyah.

These letters are very personal letters. During her lifetime we would have shied away from prying into her correspondence—and thus into her inner thoughts. Today, so many years after her death, these letters make us re-live our own memories. Those of us who knew her, adored and loved her, discover in them new dimensions and unknown aspects of her personality. Henrietta Szold's letters make us understand her more and understand ourselves better.

Through Henrietta Szold and my work with her in the service of Youth Aliyah, I had my first introduction to Hadassah. You could not be with Henrietta Szold and not learn about Hadassah. It is very fitting that this correspondence is published for Hadassah's Diamond Jubilee.

Those who were involved with Youth Aliyah were mostly very deeply involved and affected. Not only were the lives of more than 200,000 children changed—their fate different—due to Youth Aliyah. The lives of everyone who helped, educated, assisted and worked in whatever capacity with Youth Aliyah and Youth Aliyah children, were transformed. Youth Aliyah is a very personal experience. Working with Henrietta Szold in Youth Aliyah made it even more so.

For all—young and old—she meant something special. She touched and affected our lives. Even today, decades after her death, those who knew her still relate to her. How often in these last years, as Treasurer of the Jewish Agency, whenever a problem came up concerning

---

Mr. Akiva Lewinsky, leading member of the Zionist Executive is Treasurer of the Jewish Agency for Israel.

vii

children, their immigration and welfare, have I asked myself what would she have done and how would she have decided. The standards set by Henrietta Szold are still the standards we measure by.

In 1933 black clouds gathered in Europe, foreshadowing the Holocaust. For the first time, Youth Aliyah became a budget item in the Jewish Agency—and what a meager sum was allocated for one of the most dramatic undertakings of the Jewish people; 18,876 Pounds Sterling—roughly equivalent to 60 to 70 thousand U.S. dollars today.

Youngsters were not yet used to the idea of leaving home on their own and going to Israel. It was a new and revolutionary concept; it was still inconceivable that this might be their very salvation and the only hope for many of their families. We had to come to grips with the idea that children could pave the way for their parents and that children could make history.

Henrietta Szold's contributions to Jewish life in the United States and in Israel were many. Hadassah's medical services in Israel—all Israel's social services—bear her imprint. But her crowning achievement was her last: Youth Aliyah. She made it the most important and original educational enterprise undertaken in our generation, and one of which Israel is still proud.

Henrietta Szold made Youth Aliyah a Movement. Children and teachers, educators and organizers, the settlements and the schools to which the children came—all were part of the Movement, with a deep sense of history and historical responsibility. A great alliance was forged between Henrietta Szold's Youth Aliyah and the pioneers of Israel. Dozens of settlements are the creation of Youth Aliyah graduates. Those who came out of the darkness which entombed the face of the earth brought living light again.

The decision to separate children from their parents was one of the most difficult she had to take. To us, who were young, it seemed such a simple and logical decision—like the time-honored credo on a sinking ship; "Save women and children first." Today I understand that she knew the dangers probably better than we did, but she knew, too, what parents meant to children and children to parents, and what poor substitutes are even very best educators and people of good will.

There could not have been a greater dilemma than the one Henrietta Szold faced in those first years—between the growing sense of urgency, and the heavy load of responsibility entailed for children whose parents had put them in her trust. Every moment counted, every opportunity lost might not be regained, and yet there is no heavier responsibility than to replace parents when there are none, or of being guardians for children whose parents are so far away. She understood fully what it meant to take charge in place of a father or a mother, as well as the weight of the trust placed in her by those who sent their children, and for whom she was Mother Israel, who would take care.

In the Summer of 1939 I went from Palestine to Berlin. I was a witness to the incredible work of Youth Aliyah in those five weeks before the outbreak of the war. Back home, I became a madrich—an educator, in Youth Aliyah at Kiryat Anavim. Then came for me ten unforgettable years, living Youth Aliyah day and night: working with many youth groups, working together with Hans Beyth—Youth Aliyah's Director, when it was still called the Bureau for Youth Aliyah. It had not yet become a fully-fledged Jewish Agency department as we know it today. I was then in almost daily contact with Henrietta Szold. I lived, like others, that unique Movement, in partnership with Israel's pioneers, conceived, carried out and developed by Henrietta Szold—the Movement of Youth Aliyah.

I shall never forget the day we went to receive the Teheran children at Athlit railway station—the first train of refugee children I had ever seen. Who knew, then, that there would be so many trains to follow in the future?

Then came the years in Turkey as Henrietta Szold's emissary, trying to save children from burning Europe. Boats came with children, small boats, over-loaded with children, and trains—sometimes with a pitiful few and sometimes, happily, with many. And then the years in afterwar Europe, where Henrietta Szold had sent me to bring our children home.

Henrietta Szold was one of the very few in pre-State Israel whom everybody addressed in the third person. She was Miss Szold—HaG'veret Szold, the great lady Szold. Nobody raised his voice in her presence. She radiated authority. This frail and gentle woman radiated strength.

Henrietta Szold had a special relationship with the pioneers of Israel. For her, the men and women building a new country and a new society represented what she believed in. This relationship was mutual. When she called upon them to be her major partner in Youth Aliyah, they answered:

"We, the people of the kibbutzim and moshavim,
shall try to do our best to fulfill the great task
she has set us.
Henrietta Szold has lifted us up. She makes us
better humans."

Henrietta Szold was a pioneer in her own special way. Her Youth Aliyah Movement was part of a historic process, part and parcel of the Zionist Movement, in its truest sense.

In the beginning of 1945 I came back from Turkey to report to her in Jerusalem. Henrietta Szold was ill and her health declining. I came to visit her in the Hadassah Hospital on Mount Scopus. She was tired and weak, but her mind was clear and alert. Her thoughts centered already on the tasks ahead, the challenges of bringing home the Remnants and making them whole again. She talked about the Jewish communities in Turkey, in Syria and in Iraq, and the dangers they would face with the realization of the Jewish State. She talked about the hard road to peace.

Henrietta Szold used to weigh every word she uttered. She probed each one for its meaning. Never did she use a word in vain.

The effort of talking made her breathing heavier. Suddenly she said to me: "I have always wondered about the connection between 'neshima' and 'neshama'—[the Hebrew words for "breathing" and for "soul"]. Now, I understand."

Reading the letters in this book, the final meeting came back to me as clearly as dozens of other memories, of her courage, her devotion to life, and her unconquerable soul.

INTRODUCTION

On March 4, 1986, Henrietta Szold was inducted into the Maryland Women's Hall of Fame. Born in 1860 the eldest child of Rabbi Benjamin and Sophie Szold, Henrietta spent the first forty-three years of her long life in Baltimore. Here her days were devoted to education, a firm foundation for her later noteworthy achievements. Following her graduation from high school, Henrietta had desired a college education above all else. She was denied that privilege due to her family's need for her salary, small as it was, from her teaching at private schools for girls.

In November 1889 a truly major interest developed for Henrietta when she organized the pioneer night school for immigrants fleeing the atrocities of the Russian Czar. The influx of East Europeans into the urban centers to which they flocked found their rapid absorption difficult. Lacking a knowledge of their new country's language, the immigrants found it hard to obtain employment. Henrietta wrote of her evening Americanization classes: "The curriculum consisted of English, English, and again English. All else was treated as collateral and subsidiary." The benefits of her undertaking have been summed up thus: "It was frequently said by many capable merchants, doctors and lawyers that they owed their success in life to this school....It is safe to say that this institution contributed more than any other single influence to make useful citizens of those thousands of Baltimore Jewish immigrants."

In 1893 Henrietta became the secretary of the Philadelphia-based Jewish Publication Society of America. In reality she acted as editor, writer, translator, annotator, compiler, proofreader and coordinating spirit for twenty-three years. In 1903, after the death of her beloved father, Henrietta moved with her mother to New York City. Rabbi Szold had raised his eldest child for a life of Jewish scholarship, so in her spare time from the Publication Society she studied Hebrew and

Talmud at the Jewish Theological Seminary.

At her home near the Seminary, Henrietta attracted a group of young intellectuals. Among them was Professor Louis Ginzberg, a native of Lithuania. Henrietta helped prepare the material and translated the several volumes of Ginzberg's scholarly *The Legends of the Jews*. Working closely together over the years they developed what Ginzberg termed "an exceptional friendship." Although thirteen years the professor's senior, Henrietta, as his devoted confidante and companion, fell in love with him.

In 1908 Louis Ginsburg visited Berlin and fell in love with a young woman to whom he proposed marriage. When he returned to New York the Seminary was agog over the news that Ginsberg had jilted such a remarkable woman as Henrietta. When her health failed her after the disruption of her relationship with Ginzberg, Henrietta, accompanied by her mother, embarked in 1909 on a recuperative trip to Palestine via the British Isles and Europe. She wrote in her diary:

> I missed him sorely in Edinburgh. I still feel bottled and corked. I cannot speak out to anyone as I did to him—nor could he to anyone as to me—that I will believe to my dying day. Why, then, did he do what he did? It rings in my ears all the time: "You will get over this"—as tho' he wanted to add, "and hurry up about it, I find the situation uncomfortable." But I am more than that, I am broken and unhappy.

In Palestine Henrietta and her mother were horrified by the poor health conditions they saw there. Mrs. Szold remarked to Henrietta that her small group of Zionistically-inclined women in New York should devote themselves to "practical" work in Palestine instead of reading papers to each other and organizing festivals. However it was not until February 24, 1912, that a handful of these women gathered in the vestry rooms of New York's Temple Emanu-El and proclaimed themselves the Hadassah Chapter of the Daughters of Zion. Shortly afterwards Henrietta was elected its first president.

The Hadassah women voted to raise funds for sending nurses to Palestine, and in January 1913 they dispatched two nurses to Jerusalem where a settlement house was rented for them. The nurses, Miss Rose Kaplan and Miss Rachel Landy, started their health work in the Meah Shearim district of the city where malnutrition and trachoma were rampant, and where a maternity hospital was an urgent need. The nurses waged a valiant fight against the ravages of poverty and disease, but money and additional trained personnel from the United States were required. The small New York group of women could not handle the job alone, so it was decided to organize sister chapters.

On March 8, 1913, Henrietta Szold lectured in Baltimore at the Madison Avenue Temple on the work of her group and its future plans. The health of the women and children in Palestine demanded the attention of American Jewish women, she told them. Hadassah's motto, "The Healing of the Daughter of My People," was based on a passage from the Book of Jeremiah. Its symbol was the pure white myrtle blossom which Henrietta had seen in Palestine on her 1909 trip. Her impassioned speech enlisted the sympathy of twenty-nine women in the audience. Two months later she returned to Baltimore and assisted in organizing the Baltimore branch of the Daughters of Zion, called "Kadimah."

Dr. Herman H. Rubenovitz, rabbi emeritus of Boston's Temple Mishkan Tefila, wrote in *The Jewish Advocate* for January 12, 1956: "It was in the social hall of this building that the immortal Henrietta Szold made her first plea for the organization of a Boston chapter of the but recently formed Hadassah." That occurred in December 1913. By the end of 1917 Hadassah had forty-seven chapters and approximately four thousand members.

Previously, in July 1916, Hadassah, under Henrietta Szold's leadership, had accepted the request of the World Zionist Organization to organize a medical unit for Palestine. It was wartime, and only three doctors were left to serve the entire city of Jerusalem. Henrietta had expended great energy trying to raise funds for the undertaking. A forty-five member Medical Unit, together with large medical and relief supplies, finally sailed under convoy in June 1918. The Unit was accompanied by Henrietta's good friend, Miss-Alice Seligsberg. The following year Hadassah established the first school hygiene clinic which would supervise the health of Jerusalem's children from pre-birth to graduation.

Henrietta's best-known career began in 1920 when in her sixtieth year she settled in Palestine to revitalize and expand its medical, educational and social services. A tireless worker, she devoted herself to the job at hand. In 1927 she was chosen to be a member of the Zionist Executive, and in 1930 was elected a member of the Vaad Leumi, the

National Council for Palestine. Her many duties demanded a fearsome pace. On the occasion of her seventieth birthday in 1930, Dr. Stephen S. Wise of the Jewish Institute of Religion conferred on her the Degree of Doctor of Laws, saying:

> Henrietta Szold, great among women, foremost among her Jewish sisters: daughter and disciple of a learned and noble teacher, Benjamin Szold, dedicated for many years to the cause of Jewish letters; and in the latest and greatest phase of her life, by a leadership of wisdom and consecration and by an example of uncompromising nobleness among the immortal rebuilders of her people's life in the land of Israel; inspiring bringer of multitudes of Jewish women, Hadassah, to the altar of high service to their people and their people's Homeland.

In 1932 Henrietta wrote from Jerusalem to her two sisters, Bertha Levin and Adele Seltzer, that she had accumulated about $2200 from two cash birthday presents. As she did not want to use the gifts for herself she had established a Rural Clinic Building Loan Fund. And with another gift of $5000 she had set up a Rural School Building Loan Fund. Adele Seltzer answered on June 12, 1932:

> How grand it sounds—"establishing" things. I never expected to see a Szold establish things, we who never owned a patch of ground, to have buildings go up from our endowments. I'm so glad they are satisfying to you. *I'm* proud if a seed I plant begins to sprout. How must it be to see something enduring arise out of one's wish and will.

Adele wrote again to Henrietta on February 24, 1933, saying that Mrs. Felix M. Warburg, daughter of banker Jacob Schiff, had returned from a visit to Palestine in a "glow" over Henrietta. "She said that you are one of the great ones in this world, who does big things with an air of doing small things, tucking yourself away in a corner and letting others make the noise."

The advent of Hitler and the Nazi triumph in Germany produced the most difficult and demanding period in Henrietta Szold's life.

YOUTH ALIYAH IS SET IN MOTION

In October 1933 Henrietta Szold was a delegate to the London conference on the German Jewish situation. She was in Berlin on the Friday of Hitler's address preceding the plebiscite of November 12 which endorsed the Nazi regime. She began to be looked upon as the leader of the attempt to rescue Jewish children from Germany—the movement which became Youth Aliyah. She wrote to her nephew, Jastrow Levin, on January 4, 1934:

> My newest field is organizing at the Palestinian end the transfer of young people between the ages of fifteen and seventeen from Germany to Palestine. Your mother may have written you that I was in Europe during the month of November and went to Berlin and Hamburg, to Amsterdam and Paris for the purpose of establishing the contact between Germany and Palestine for the benefit of the youth movement. Next week I expect to motor through the country for the purpose of looking into the possibilities of settling groups of juveniles, at the adolescent age, in our rural settlements. In a few weeks the first group is expected to come to one of the largest settlements, at Ein Harod, in the Valley of Jezreel. It's a great responsibility, one of those puzzling problems of education which age has not enabled me to solve to my own satisfaction.
>
> I ought to have nothing but appreciation for the privilege of being able to work as hard as I do at the age of seventy-three. And let me whisper to you that sometimes I don't believe the calendar. I often don't feel seventy-three. Indeed, sometimes I feel a child. I thought when I was a child, and even after I grew into womanhood, and even into mature womanhood, that age brings wisdom. And here

1

I am, well beyond three score and ten, and the world and its complexities continue to be the same puzzle, engaging and baffling at the same time, as they were back in that remote epoch when I began to realize that this is a world.

On February 19 of that year the first contingent of forty-three children arrived at Haifa on the S.S. *Martha Washington*. Henrietta met the group at the dock and escorted them to Kibbutz Ein Harod.

Henrietta's sister, Adele Seltzer, wrote to her from Danbury, Connecticut:

> The work you are doing for the German refugees surely is not so immeasurably finer than what you have done for health and education and all the rest. Perhaps it is more spectacular. America seems to be thrilled by it. People who know you have always spoken to me of your wonderful doings, but now strangers tell me they hear all around of Miss Szold's marvellous achievements for the refugee children.
>
> As I read you poetic letters of the arrival of the German children, of their bursting into song, of their crying *entzuckend*—"delightful"—of the simple life into which they are to be fitted, I am actually filled with a glow. But then—the other side of the coin. Not the wayward youth you mention, but England, perfidious Albion, treacherous, arrogant, imperialistic England. Do you purposely never mention the political situation—the rising nationalism of the Arabs, the restriction of immigration, the deceitful lion—or isn't the future menace to your Jewish "homeland" as grim as it seems to me?

Henrietta answered that the situation was indeed grim. England had gone back on her word to the Jews, and Arab nationalism was increasing, a double worry. What disturbed her even more was the constant labor disputes and political quarrels among the Jews: "Our political divisions here are deplorable."

On October 19, 1934, Henrietta wrote to her sisters that she had "survived" her own Hebrew speech and the other ceremonies connected with the cornerstone-laying of the Rothschild Hadassah-University Hospital and Medical School on Mount Scopus three days earlier. She was chairman of the event which was broadcast to the Hadassah Convention in America. She confessed that she had been "thrilled" by the idea of broadcasting to London and New York. The expectant waiting until the red light flashed on to announce that connection between the two distant continents had been established she found "awesome."

Adel wrote from Connecticut on November 13:

> Like Bertha I listened, or tried to listen, to your voice from Mt. Scopus, along with Mr. and Mrs. Warburg in their home. In spite of their $2,500 instrument the static was awful. You just went boom, boom, boom. Some words from the next speaker came through. Then, for that child of luck, Judah Leon Magnes, the static cleared away completely, and his tones rang as mellifluous as from the pulpit of Temple Emanu-El.

Dr. Magnes, formerly rabbi of New York's Temple Emanu-El, was then chancellor of the Hebrew University on Mount Scopus.

Henrietta's birthday on December 21, 1934, was extensively celebrated. A week later she wrote to her nephew, Benjamin Levin, from her apartment in Jerusalem's Hotel Eden:

> My birthday caused others a great deal more excitement than it would have caused me, if I didn't now have to write dozens of letters of acknowledgment of cables, letters, flowers, and other gifts. Last Friday a stream of visitors began to pour in and it continued to pour until Saturday night, and dribbled all week. I must reveal the cause of all this public attention. I myself could not explain why on my seventy-fourth birthday, not the number of years usually marked by wide celebration, there should come, beginning with the first day of December, cable after cable. Late in the month the explanation came in a Release to the Press by Hadassah in America. They were having a Membership Campaign for 7400 members, 100 for each one of my years. I was convenient propaganda material! I wish I could make Hadassah write my "thank you" letters.

Thirteen days earlier Henrietta had visited Kibbutz Kinneret (Ha-Shomer Ha-Zair, a settlement belonging to the leftist wing of the Palestine labor movement). Her letter to her nephew continued:

> I found things in a much better state of preparedness for the German young people than my former visit had given me reason to expect. This time I went up with a group of 62 children from Germany. In the evening of the day of arrival there was a great reception. At

Deganiah A, to which the residents of all the settlements in the region came, there was feasting and singing and dancing, and of course speechmaking.

One of the speakers was Yisrael Galili, a young Ukranian Jew who in 1930 had helped found Kibbutz Naan near Ramla. He became head of the Haganah, the defense group of Palestinian settlers, later incorporated into the Israeli Army. ''Galili spoke particularly well, ''Henrietta commented. ''He likened the Youth Aliyah to the Children's Crusade, only to bring out the fundamental differences.''

On the last day of January 1935, Henrietta had to go to Tel Aviv in a bad storm and returned to Jerusalem in a worse storm. ''The wind blew me away and knocked me down, none too softly,'' she wrote. ''I wish I might have had a photograph of myself flying through the air.'' She had gone to Tel Aviv to give a talk on the structure of the Keneset Israel, the union of the Jewish communities of Palestine, to a large group of newly-arrived German women. Henrietta found them to be intelligent and avid for information about the land to which they had come. Since they could not understand the language of their Palestinian associates nor read the newspapers, they had to wait for information about what was going on around them until the *Judische Runschau*, a Jewish review, reached them from Germany. But as Henrietta was fluent in German she was able to answer many of their questions.

Henrietta was constantly on the go regardless of weather, meeting the young people coming from Germany. She wrote on February 22:

> I was again out of town for three days, this time to welcome twenty-six new arrivals of the Youth Immigration. I accompanied the sixteen who were destined for Mishmar Ha-Emek, and spent the night there, sleeping in a barracks which serves as the ''hotel'' of the place. The room is furnished with all one needs, including running (or rather trickling) water. There was a welcoming with speeches, nuts and fruits—good speeches at that—and of course the Horah, the inevitable. Mishmar Ha-Emek is the best-ordered Kvutzah I know, and their attitude towards life and particularly education is most satisfactory. But such mud and such incessant rain!

American tourists arrived steadily and in droves, all of them anxious to meet Henrietta. Dr. L. Hess, a dentist, and his wife from Baltimore were among them. They were in Jerusalem for only two days, and Henrietta found it hard to discuss with such tourists the broad spectrum and convolutions of Palestinian life. So with Dr. Hess she talked of the "good old times" in Baltimore: "I was amazed myself—as he was—at the memories and names I pulled out of the storehouse where they had been gathering dust these many years."

American tourists consumed a considerable amount of her time. Her friend for some sixty years, Dr. Harry Friedenwald, a prominent Baltimore ophthalmologist, and his daughter, Mrs. Julia Strauss, stayed at the Hotel Eden and asked Henrietta to share their table. Julia, president of the Baltimore Chapter of Hadassah, wrote to her husband, Myer Strauss:

> It made the trip additionally stimulating to be privileged daily to enjoy the society of Miss Henrietta, to drink of her deep wisdom and to wonder at her selfless devotion to her two jobs which keep her actively engaged from 7:30 every day, all day and almost every evening, excepting *Shabbat*. She is a marvel, she would be remarkable were she my age, but I can never understand how she is equal to it at 74½ years of age—a most extraordinary personality!

Henrietta was being urged to go to Germany, Holland and Poland in the interests of Youth Aliyah. There was to be a conference in Amsterdam called by the various European groups raising funds for the Youth Aliyah. The movement was to be extended to include young Poles as well as Germans. By mid-July she had not yet consented to going. "I always find it hard to mobilize myself," she said. "I foresee, however, that I shall not be able to resist—the pressure promises to be great." By the end of the month the die was cast: she was to leave on August 14.

At Lucerne Henrietta stayed at the Hôtel Schweizerhof while she attended the 19th World Zionist Congress. Chaim Weizmann, president of the Organization, and other prominent Zionists listened attentively as Henrietta addressed the Congress. At the conclusion of her speech she was tendered an ovation. The Congress formed a committee on social service work in Palestine and voted it funds.

Next came the Amsterdam conference which enlarged the Youth Aliyah to include thousands of young people from Lithuania, France, Poland, and Carpathian Russia—a gigantic task. Berlin followed Amsterdam on Henrietta's itinerary. There she was immersed in "misery and sorrow." She had arrived at Berlin at almost the very moment when Hitler was delivering his speech at Nuremberg. And while Henrietta was making an address to a Jewish group, she had heard the stormtroopers yell: "Jude, verecke!"—"Death to the Jews!"

Henrietta's reception by various Jewish groups was overwhelming. Never had such homage been paid her. Even the little children knew who she was. "There would be much to write, particularly about my experiences in Berlin," she told a nephew. "To be there was living history, the sort of history one reads about but does not envisage as a present possibility. At present, in Vienna, I am being petted and loved by a swarm of relatives." She hoped to arrive in Palestine on October 15: "I am afraid to think of the sea of work into which I shall have to plunge after my prolonged absence."

Henrietta's nephew, Benjamin Szold Levin, had emigrated to Palestine with his wife Sarah. He wrote from Jerusalem to his brother Jastrow at Baltimore on November 7, 1935, that he had noticed on his Aunt Henrietta's desk a letter with a stamp bearing the picture of Vladimir Jabotinsky. In 1925 Jabotinsky had organized the World Union of Zionist Revisionists, an extremist Zionist group which demanded drastic and even militant revisions of the Zionist program. The Revisionists used the Jabotinsky stamps instead of the Jewish National Fund Stamps. Benjamin wrote:

> I asked Aunt Henrietta why Revisionists wrote to her at all. It turned out that although the Revisionists have withdrawn from the Zionist organization they nevertheless want her to take an interest in a Revisionist Youth Aliyah. So do the Agudat Israel, which you know is an orthodox organization outside the Zionist body. The Agudat Israel are handicapped by their many worries over details. They want a German Youth Aliyah too, but they want a guarantee that boys and girls will be kept strictly separate, a thing the Zionists find it practically impossible to do. The Agudists refuse to use Hadassah medical facilities in Jerusalem because there are female nurses! One of them would pass out if a young nurse tried to sponge him or take his temperature.
>
> Preparations are already underway for Aunt Henrietta's 75th birthday.

In December Henrietta sailed for New York where she was met by her sister, Adele Seltzer. To avoid publicity Henrietta had slipped quietly from the steamer and motored with Adele to Baltimore. There they stayed at the home of their sister, Bertha Levin, at 2104 Chelsea Terrace. The Baltimore *Sun* reporter noted that Miss Szold looked fifteen years younger than she was, walked with a buoyant step, and displayed frequent flashes of humor. She said that she did not want to think of age as she had a great deal of work ahead of her. And recalling her past in Baltimore she told the reporter: "It was exactly fifty-two years ago that I received the first Russian immigrants to reach here down at a local pier."

Since Henrietta's birthday fell on Shabbat, rabbis in various cities devoted part of their services to extolling her work. At Baltimore's Chizuk Amuno Synagogue a special program was presided over by Julia Strauss, president of the local Hadassah chapter. Mrs. Emil Crockin, first president of Baltimore Hadassah, reviewed her career, while Dr. Harry Friedenwald delivered the main address. "Dr. Harry," as he was called, devoted the first portion of his birthday talk to a nostalgic word picture of the early home life of the Szold family where he had spent so many happy hours. "What less than an *Isha Gedolah*, a great woman, shall we call her," Dr. Harry concluded, "who has provided, not for one nor for a hundred, but for a thousand youths, and who is restoring them to a new life of hope and dignity ....May we not say to her as Mordecai spoke to Esther: 'And who knoweth whether thou are not come to royal estate for such a time as this?' "

Other Zionist leaders participated in an international broadcast lauding her endeavors. Henrietta herself took no part in the celebration. She thanked Dr. Harry Friedenwald by mail: "I am relieved that I was not present when you spoke thus. It would have been beyond my powers of self-control to listen without betraying emotion that is not for the public eye."

Praise poured in on Henrietta from many directions. General Sir Arthur Wauchope, British High Commissioner for Palestine, wrote to Mrs. Tamar de Sola Pool, president of Hadassah:

> I have full sympathy with Hadassah in their natural desire to celebrate Miss Szold's 75th birthday. All who know Miss Szold's achievement in Palestine in the cause of promoting health and happiness know its high value. All who know Miss Szold trust she may live for many years and be able to continue that good work.

Menachem Ussishkin, for many years president of the Jewish National Fund, wrote that the 19th Zionist Congress at Lucerne had "unanimously and enthusiastically" resolved to establish and to name after Miss Szold an agricultural settlement in Palestine to mark the occasion of her 75th birthday. The decision was unique as not a single settlement, suburb, or street in Palestine then bore the name of a Jewess:

"Miss Szold thus has the privilege of inaugurating a new chapter in the history of Jewish womanhood in our generation." And Meir Dizengoff, founder and first mayor of Tel Aviv, wrote: "Henrietta Szold's work is particularly distinguished for its absence of any bias or partisanship. She stands above any class or political party."

At Baltimore Henrietta relished her visit with her two sisters. She was driven to Johns Hopkins Hospital to welcome a new arrival, tiny Betsy Levin, the first grandchild of her sister Bertha. Betsy was born just four days after the "twin" birthdays of Henrietta and Bertha.

And Henrietta reestablished ties with former classmates from Western High School, and with colleagues of the Women's Literary Club of Baltimore. Henrietta's name appears on the first membership list of the club, along with other talented women including Mrs. Sidney Lanier, wife of the poet; Mrs. John F. Goucher, who with her husband were among the founders of Goucher College; Annie Leakin Sioussat, the historian; and poet Lizette Woodward Reese. The Club, founded for the purpose of holding literary discussions, was the first of its kind in Baltimore and the second in the nation. Henrietta, had she chosen to pursue such a career, could have been a leading essayist. "What Judaism Has Done For Women," was the theme of her paper delivered before the Women's Parliament at the Columbian World's Fair in 1895. Her essay, "A Century of Jewish Thought," written the following year, was excerpted in Dr. Joseph H. Hertz's *A Book of Jewish Thoughts*. And the *Jewish Encyclopedia* of 1904 contained sixteen short essays by Henrietta on the lives of prominent Jewish women of various periods and countries, plus a scholarly history of Baltimore, and an account of the Jewish Publication Society. Much of her writing was directed toward the redemption of Palestine.

Before she embarked at New York aboard the S.S. *Lafayette*, Henrietta was greeted in New York's City Hall by Mayor Fiorella LaGuardia. The Mayor thanked her by saying, "If I, the child of poor immigrant parents, am today Mayor of New York, giving you the freedom of our city, it is because of you. Half a century ago you initiated that instrument of American democracy, the evening school for the immigrant...."

Henrietta sailed, taking with her the pledge that Hadassah's 50,000 members would support the Youth Aliyah; they raised over $100,000. And Hadassah planned to plant a forest in her name on Mount Scopus.

Henrietta's time aboard the S.S. *Lafayette* was devoted to acknowledging the many birthday greetings. Her sister Adele wrote to her from New York, "Hurry up and get to be seventy-six. Or will another birthday, even if it does not make a decimal year, stir things up again? I can't forget the painful sight of you so weary, so weary amid all the celebrating.''

Henrietta Szold in
Berlin, November 1933.

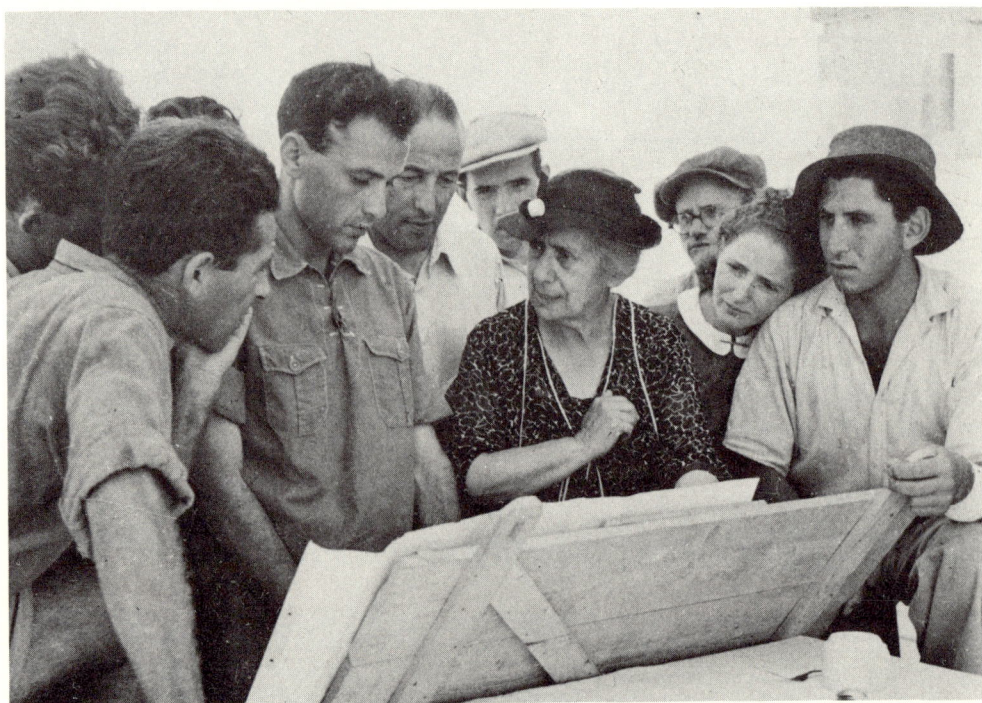

Making plans for a new youth installation. Hans Beyth, Miss Szold's
assistant, stand behind her right shoulder.

Hans Beyth, 1935

Henrietta Szold, July 1936

New group of German children at Geva, Palestine, planting 10,000 trees. In center, bending down, Henrietta Szold plants a tree. Photo taken in 1936 by Dr. Jonas Friedenwald of Baltimore.

ARAB RIOTS PLAGUE PALESTINE

In its issue for January 1, 1936, the *Nation* magazine listed in its Honor Roll Henrietta Szold, along with Secretary of State Cordell Hull, Senator Hugo L. Black of Alabama, Roger N. Baldwin and the American Civil Liberties Union, writer Maxwell Anderson, and playwright Clifford Odets, among others. Her commendation read: "Henrietta Szold, who at seventy-five years of age, after a crowded lifetime of work in behalf of the oppressed Jews of all countries, is head of the Youth Aliyah movement which has already transferred almost a thousand German-Jewish children to Palestine and settled them on the land."

Chaim Weizmann, first president of the State of Israel, would write in his autobiography, *Trial and Error*,* about his chairmanship of the Central Bureau for the Settlement of German Jews:

> My work ran parallel with that of the Youth Aliyah, which was head-ed by one of the most remarkable figures in modern Jewish history—Henrietta Szold....In the founding of Hadassah, the American Women's Zionist Organization, she had made an im-mense contribution to the social and political development of the Jewish Homeland; and to climax her work and that of her organiza-tion, she had settled in Palestine, where her energy, wisdom and devotion were an inspiration to the community. At an age well beyond that of usual retirement from public life, she undertook and carried through with magnificent effectiveness the direction of Youth Aliyah, one of the most important Zionist tasks....

---

* *(Philadelphia*, Jewish Publication Society, *1949), Vol. II, 349-350.*

Hadassah, as a seventy-fifth birthday present to its founder had commissioned writer Marvin Lowenthal to piece together the story of her life from the fragments of her writings. Henrietta's sister, Adele Seltzer, had been busy with the project. She wrote on February 25, 1936:

> I wonder if you realize that since I came to New York I have been spending several hours a day, not regularly, but frequently, at the Hadassah office, arranging and reading your correspondence, with gaps, to your "Dear Sisters" since 1909. They make thrilling reading, and I have come to the conclusion that letters should be read when they fall into the category of history and lose their character of gossip at the moment. If everyone else in the world weren't thumping into you that you are a "great" person, I should tell you that they are the letters of a great person.

Ever since her return from America, Henrietta had been on the go. She attributed her ability to maintain her exhausting pace to the fact that she kept the Sabbath and had a cast-iron stomach. She wrote to her nephew Benjamin on March 19:

> I had to rush off to visit Youth Aliyah groups in the Emek. I am making Afulah my center. Tomorrow I start out as early as may be, which won't be very early I am sure, because I am to wait for Dr. Jonas Friedenwald who is coming up from Jerusalem to join me on tomorrow's expedition.

Dr. Jonas Friedenwald, son of Henrietta's old friend, Dr. Harry, had come to Palestine to deliver a series of lectures on ophthalmology at the Hebrew University. He was to travel with Henrietta through the Emek to see a group of German refugee children, who had already received their initial training at Ein Harod, welcome the second group arriving at the settlement. Henrietta reported:

> I waited at Afula until Mr. Hans Beyth, my wonderful assistant in the Youth Work, came up from Jerusalem with Jonas Friedenwald. First we went to Kfar Gideon, to which it had been suggested we send a group of young people. From there we went to David, to which twenty children had come. For Jonas' sake I went over the place thoroughly—storehouses, stables, sheep hurdles, poultry houses, workshops, kitchen, every nook and corner—and found I

was as much interested as though I had planned the circuit for my own sake. The group there comes from Czechoslovakia. It's strange—I do get a home-feeling with people that come from our parents' home. It happens, too, that the youth group they have adopted is a particularly well-bred set of young people.

At Kibbutz Geva the new group of German boys and girls had each planted a young sapling in a stretch of twelve acres prepared for a future woodland of ten thousand trees to bear Henrietta's name. They had left one space vacant, and when Henrietta arrived with Jonas Friedenwald, the youths formed a procession to witness her solitary tree-planting. Jonas snapped a photo of Henrietta bending over to plant the sapling, while one youth held for her a bucket of water. The young immigrants, whose individual trees would bear their names, undoubtedly felt rooted to the land by this their first symbolic act.

Henrietta's cousin, Arnold Schaar from Vienna, had arrived at Jerusalem and requested her to reserve for him a room at the Hotel Eden. Henrietta doubted whether Arnold could spend a night at a kibbutz or even a village because he demanded all the comforts of civilization: "he is not able to stand any sort of inconvenience." She wrote to her sisters on April 2, 1936:

> I must tell you about the gift brought me by Arnold from Lottie Kien—a gold ducat of the 1848 minting, which our father gave to Lottie's mother, Aunt Minna, as a wedding gift, on his own wedding day which was also Aunt Minna's. Uncle Heinrich Schaar had a beautifully carved mother-of-pearl tiny box made for it. The ducat itself had been acquired with the first installment of Papa's salary, sent to him by the Baltimore Oheb Shalom Congregation, presumably to enable him to meet his travelling expenses across land and sea. The ducat, as you see, was never touched for a base everyday use, though probably there were occasions and temptations to change it. I don't see how Lottie could bear to part with it.

On April 19 news went out over the wires from Palestine of the widespread Arab revolt sponsored by an improvised ARab High Committee. During the first four days of unrest 23 people were killed and 190 wounded. The Arabs planned to stir up trouble in Jerusalem for the 24th of the month. They urged villagers to come into the city and gather at the Aksa Mosque in hopes of starting riots and demonstrations. A general strike was proclaimed which, except for the closing of shops, was relatively ineffective. This had produced rising tension and concern in the Jewish community which felt that the British High Commissioner, Sir Arthur Wauchope, was not exercising the energy and determination in the situation one might have reason to expect from a soldier. Yet the government was making preparations to put down any trouble, and members of Yisrael Galili's Haganah, the Jewish self-defense organization, were everywhere quietly apparent. People in Jerusalem had been advised to stay indoors until it was clear which way the wind was blowing. For several months past acts of terrorism had been occurring on all roads, and Jews on busses were threatened and one Jew shot dead.

To Henrietta the Arab question was the central and chief problem to be solved by Palestinian Jews. She considered it the acid test of the Jews' worthiness as a people from the point of view of their ethical system. She wrote to her nephew Benjamin on April 24:

> To my regret my experience among Jews and their attitude towards Arabs has been quite the same as yours. I have witnessed scenes that made my blood boil. You tell of the scene you witnessed when a Jewish shopkeeper kicked an Arab boy. I am told that such acts in Tel Aviv last Saturday after the demonstration were the immediate causes of the riot on Sunday. Venders of fruit were beaten up and sent back to Jaffa bruised and bleeding. Of course, the causes for the disturbances lie deeper. They lie in the deep bed of race antagonisms and national ideals and resentments. They come out in the discussion of the Legislative Council, the Parlimentary debates about it, the Land Laws legislation, etc. And the match that is set to all this fuel is in the hands of the agitator. In consideration of the agitator, the question arises whether the studied neutrality of the Government serves a good purpose.

Arab agitators continued to plot incitement by means of a general strike. Fires had been set to houses, shops, and machinery, while hundreds of fruit-bearing trees and saplings were uprooted in that tree-less country. At Ein Harod alone, 550 orange and grapefruit trees were destroyed, and the woodland at Mishmar Ha-Emek set afire. On May 8 the Arab Supreme Committee called for civil disobedience. Unless the British Government stopped the immigration of Jews, forbade land sales to Jews, and established a national Arab government by the 15th, the strike would be continued and the Arab population refuse to pay taxes.

Henrietta wrote from the Hotel Eden on May 8:

> The fears of the Arabs are not groundless. Our peaceful endeavors in our own behalf are undeniably pressing them to the wall. The first requisite is that we should be honest and sincere in our desire to live on terms of equality with them in this land upon which we have a shadowy (in the political sense) but a strong sentimental claim, and upon which they have the claim which is phrased: possession is nine points of the law. The second requisite is that we should, in the name of justice and true brotherliness, be ready to sustain losses and make compromises. The rest will come of itself. Sincerity and justice first—practical steps in a thousand directions the outcome. That is a hard path to travel. It is the only one for us. It was heartening to me this week that at the meeting of the Vaad Leumi I heard for the first time in public, exhortations to a course such as I have outlined, and there was no voiced opposition.

The bombings, murders and destruction continued, as did the terror. "I must say I like the mediaeval custom of curfew," Henrietta declared on May 22. "It is a wonderful protection against intrusions and interruptions, at least during certain hours." Jerusalem had experienced a bad week, and the suffering was great, particularly among the Jews living in the Old City. There was widespread unemployment, and there was hunger and fear. Hundreds had left the Old City and were camping wherever they could find space and tolerance. And there were no funds for relief. "As for myself and my safety, staying at home is no safeguard," Henrietta admitted on May 31. "Stray bullets penetrate to every corner." It looked as though there would be weeks if not months of continued guerrilla warfare. "We Jews must continue at any price to exercise self-restraint. It's our only chance." Henrietta had always suspected that the Jews were not genuinely desirous of finding the ways of peace and justice. "The recent discussions I have heard have made it plain to me that we incline to desire the displacement of the Arab from the land." Indeed, her notions of Zionist policy were undergoing severe shocks in many respects.

When the terrorist acts continued, Henrietta wrote on June 5:

> It's all one can think about. To be sure, I go on steadily—more than steadily—with my work, but subconsciously always the other ugly thing occupies me. The Jews are admirable. Yet I wish they were a little more admirable.For instance, while I understand and even

have not a little sympathy with the joy over the capture of a port at Tel Aviv, I cannot but wish that the manifestations of joy were not so close akin to hatred. On account of such joy, which means in my opinion, still further removal from an understanding between the two peoples, I see the future dark. All the insistence one reads in the editorials that the riots and murders and spoliations only strengthen our determination not to allow ourselves to be dislodged is disquieting from the ethical point of view. Is there no Arab side to the problem? Is it not our business to see the Arab side, too, and think out the necessary adjustment? Or am I a wishy-washy Liberal?

Six days later Henrietta confided to her nephew Benjamin:

One cannot ward off anxiety when one hears of such outrages as were just now reported, the bomb explosion in a train wounding seventeen Jews, all Arabs having left the train a moment before it happened. It's gruesome. And the destruction of trees, and the general impoverishment among Arabs and Jews. It is amazing that one can nevertheless go on with life's routine as most of us do. As for the streets of Jerusalem, I doubt whether they are any more dangerous than any other place in the country. There is no protection against ambush and guerrilla attacks. The worst of the business, the two worst, is that the end is not in sight, for the strike fund is said to be enormous, and what will come after, dictated by the hatred that has been engendered, is also unforetellable.

Benjamin Levin and his wife were living in a settlement east of Tel Aviv, called Petah Tikva, ''Door of Hope,'' a center of citrus culture. This oldest of Jewish agricultural settlements in Palestine had been founded in 1878 by Jews from Jerusalem who believed that tending the soil would redeem the people of Israel. Benjamin wrote to his brother Jastrow on June 9:

History is being made in the spot. During seven weeks the Arabs have killed nearly 30 Jews and destroyed much Jewish property including many thousands of orange trees. The Jews have probably not killed one Arab and have not destroyed Arab property. The Jewish press has been fairly moderate in tone. However, Aunt Henrietta, whose New England conscience makes her strain to see the Arab side, has praised the Jewish attitude, with reservations.

Over 20 Arabs have been killed—all by English policement. Petah Tikva is about the safest place in the country. An Arab who walks through the colony today puts on a slouch hat more or less Western in style in order to be less conspicuous. Before the disturbances no Arab ever wore anything on his head but a fez, shawl, or small, brimless cap.

The Arab strike has completed its seventh week. It was a very foolish idea because it gives the Jews just what they want. Now at last there is Jewish labor in the pardessim of Petah Tikva—1000 Jewish orange workers against 100 Arabs. The Arab economic boycott forces all Jews to buy Jewish farm products, a thing that "patriots" had been doing anyway. The strike of the Jaffa boatmen and dock workers has been answered by the new pier at Tel Aviv. This is a knockout blow because, if all Jewish passengers and goods destined for southern Palestine come in at Tel Aviv, Jaffa will amount to little as a port. The Haifa stevedores have taken this lesson to heart and have remained at work. Many of them belong to the International Labor Federation of Arabs and Jews sponsored by the Histadrut. The striking Arabs have sent down hundreds of agitators to stop their work but without success.

Henrietta's devoted young secretary, Emma Ehrlich, was preparing to sail for the United States toward the end of July. Henrietta wondered how she would meet her obligations and responsibilities during Emma's six months' absence. It was not only Emma's actual large amount of work she would miss, but also her managerial ability, good judgment, and knowledge of every detail of Henrietta's various undertakings, personal and official. Emma was also Henrietta's "memory."

In August Henrietta was kept busy traveling to Tel Aviv where she was in charge of liquidating the camp of the Jewish refugees from Jaffa. Following the disorders on April 19, over 10,500 Jews had fled to Tel Aviv from Jaffa where they were being shot down due to lack of adequate police protection. A couple of thousand were taken in by relatives, but the public had to make arrangements for 9000 in 85 camps. The refugees could not return to their former homes in Jaffa, and during the summer some were able to establish themselves in Tel Aviv or elsewhere. But by August 4, 650 people were still camped out in vacant houses, halls, synagogues and in tents. A large sum of money was raised to resettle these people, comprising about 962 families: half came from a popular collection, and half from the government which insisted that the camps be liquidated within three months.

Toward the end of August Henrietta was returning from Tel Aviv, and when she alighted from her convoyed omnibus she ran into a large crowd attending the funeral of Professor Levi Billig who taught Arabic language and literature at the Hebrew University. The London-born professor had been sitting at his desk poring over an Arabic manuscript when a bullet crashed through his iron shutter and tore off the back of his head. He was only thirty-nine. Henrietta wrote on August 22: "Poor Professor Billig! The mildest, kindliest man that ever drew breath. I wonder whether there are methods of crushing the rebellion that the government might, but does not want to use."

CHAPTER 3

THE WORK CONTINUES
UNDER TRYING CONDITIONS

"This noon I met the three American Senators," Henrietta wrote on August 28, 1936. "They came with their secretary, Mr. Don Levine, to the Vaad Leumi to ask questions." The three senators, Royal S. Copeland of New York, Warren R. Austin of Vermont, and Daniel O. Hastings of Delaware, constituted an unofficial Senatorial Commission sponsored by the Hearst newspapers. Their mission was to gather information on the ever-increasing Arab-Jewish conflict. Possibly they could act as mediators. Isaac Don Levine, a Russian-born Jewish foreign correspondent, acted as their special aide and adviser.

The group had arrived at Jerusalem on August 25, and found the city gates reinforced with barbed wire fences and guarded by armed patrols. Curfew stopped most movement in the city promptly at seven o'clock each evening. Although the party had been warned by the British officials not to visit the Jewish communities, they came to ask questions of the Vaad Leumi—National Council of Palestine—the official body representing Palestine Jewry in lcoal affairs. Henrietta had her picture taken with the three senators, Don Levine. and Itzhak Ben-Zvi, president of the Vaad Leumi, and later president of Israel. Senator Copeland wrote in his report:

> There are really two strikes going on in Palestine. One is conducted by Arab terrorists who throw bombs and snipe at passers-by in the streets and on the highways. The other is conducted silently by the Mandatory Government of Palestine against the proper administration of justice.

18

Certain Arab leaders had protested to the senators that the Jewish settlers were displacing the Arabs. But was Jewish immigration the cause of Arab emigration? Senator Copeland's report continued: "Before the war, the Arabs were migrating from Palestine by the thousands....Over 100,000 Arabs from the surrounding countries entered Palestine as immigrants since the beginnings of the Jewish development of the country..."*

Henrietta had met with the senators and Don Levine at noon. She was scheduled to meet them again at tea, along with their wives. "I don't feel much in the humor for social functions after the happenings of this morning in Jerusalem; nor is the atmosphere of the end-strike negotiations conducive to peace of mind," she wrote. "I wish the tension were over, and we knew the worst. This rumor-mongering is beastly."

Benjamin Levin had settled at Kfar Syrkin, a moshav east of Petah Tikva. He wrote to his brother Jastrow on September 10, 1936:

> Since becoming a member of Kfar Syrkin, or Syrkinville, I have gone out two nights a week on guard. There are half a dozen uniformed special officers, called locally by the Arabic name "ghaffirim," who are paid by the government either in full or partly, and who bear army rifles. Nobody else is supposed to have anything more than a hunting gun holding one or two bullets. This law, however, is like the old Prohibition Law. A man gets 8 years for bearing arms without permission but, since the government does not carry out its share of the task of making life and property secure, neither Jews nor Arabs feel great respect for this law. The unarmed guards are stationed at intervals along the border in couples. They have whistles and blow thrice if they see or hear anything suspicious. Most nights have been quiet, affording nothing more than a splendid chance to study astronomy.
>
> However last week there was a diversion. It was twelve o'clock midnight and I was resting on the porch of a house ready to relieve the guard at 12:30 and take the second watch till dawn, when suddenly "bang! whiz!", a bullet whistled through the air. A gang was firing on the moshav from across the railroad tracks, using the railroad embankment as breastworks. The ghaffirim returned the fire and for one and a half hours there was heavy firing. It was my first experience of being under fire. The wife in the house where I

Isaac Don Levine, Eyewitness to History *(N.Y.: Hawthorn Books, 1973), 153.

was got out of bed and stretched out on the floor, as did her children. In the dark the flash of bullets could be clearly seen. The whistle of the bullets through the air was a new sound to me. Shortly after 12:30 I went out on guard. I crawled on my belly from the house to the edge of the field where there is a shallow dugout 10 or 15 inches deep used by the watch. Here I lay on my belly, peeping over the edge occasionally. The firing started again. Presently, however, the English police came down from the Ras-el-Ain railroad station with machine guns. "B-r-r-r-ump!" A spray of bullets was sent over our heads into the fields across the tracks. Another time and yet another machine gun rattled. In the dark they could not aim exactly at the bandits, but the spray was too heavy for the gang and they went away. No damage had been done to the colony, and, so far as anyone knew, none to the gangsters either.

It is interesting that the colonies have stood firm. Not one colony has been penetrated by armed Arabs, not even the kibbutz of Kurdish Jews consisting of a few mud huts and tents. This is the first time in history since the Diaspora that Jewish settlements have been entirely successful in resisting attacks. The ghaffirim are in fact a sort of Jewish army or "national guard." As a matter of fact, they frequently hold a colony safe until police or soldiers come up to reinforce them. On the other hand, the mixed cities in Palestine are still more of a "Golus" than an "Eretz Yisrael." In Jaffa, Hebron, the old city of Jerusalem, Tiberias and Safed the Jews have been unable to defend themselves and thousands of them are refugees in Tel Aviv, where Aunt Henrietta is busying herself with them. This is because the British have not allowed the city Jews to defend themselves.

One of the chief Arab sports is to snipe at chauffeurs of omnibuses from behind trees or rocks. Yet the chauffeurs have gone on bravely with their work, and passengers have not been lacking either. Aunt Henrietta contributes her bit of heroism by continuing to ride to Tel Aviv and Haifa in spite of firing on buses and the devilish traps of bombs placed on railroad tracks.

Henrietta was indeed heroic as, accompanied by her assistant, Hans Beyth, she was driven back and forth by her young chauffeur, Oscar Eckhaus, who kept a revolver carefully hidden under his seat. Henrietta loved nature and often asked Eckhaus to stop and let her examine a flower or tree. On the winding road from Ramleh to Lydda stood an ancient sycamore whose gnarled, spreading branches she often stopped to admire. Passersby came to call it "Etz Szold"—the Szold tree.

Henrietta's living room and small outside balcony were filled with plants which she tended with affectionate care. In earlier days she had been a member of the Baltimore Botany Club, and together with other nature enthusiasts had explored Druid Hill Park and the woods and meadows around the city for botanical specimens. She had insisted, however, that the club's members study botany seriously and not make it merely a social occasion.

Despite the worry of sniping, bombing and murder, Henrietta continued her work. She wrote from the Hotel Eden on September 11:

> Last Tuesday I took the early morning train for Haifa in order to meet the largest group of German boys and girls we have yet had, one hundred and five. They came in on a French steamer early in the morning. However in spite of the slowness of the train I reached Haifa in time to see them all and be with them for hours. The boat had brought in nearly a thousand passengers. It took a long time to discharge them.

Henrietta was of the opinion that the large group of German Youth Aliyah children might be the last batch to come for some time. Recently the British Government, despite much pleading on the part of Youth Aliyah, had granted only 100 Youth Certificates instead of the 450 asked for.

"In a sense life is not varied these days—it's thinking about Arab-Jewish relations without conclusions, and travelling to Tel Aviv," she wrote to Benjamin on September 25. "This week, indeed, there were two trips to Tel Aviv, on Tuesday for the refugees' business, and on Thursday for the Dizengoff funeral." Meir Dizengoff, the builder and first mayor of the city, had sent Henrietta a letter only a few days before he died. Three months younger than she, he wrote that he expected that by the time she reached eighty she would be mother to all the children of Palestine. Henrietta described the funeral:

> It was impressive, chiefly because it was a demonstration, in another form, of the restraint which we Jews, usually subjective, aggressive, unmindful of forms, are capable. Those tens of thousands maintained a solemn silence, a decorum of spirit, which illustrated to the eye and ear what we demonstrated all through these terrible months through a spirit of self-restraint which the more I think of it, the more admirable and significant it seems to me.

Henrietta had received world from Emma Ehrlich that she was attending the Hadassah Convention in Philadelphia, and from there was to go on a two weeks' visit to the Levins at Baltimore. "She seems to be having a breathless time," Henrietta exclaimed on October 18. "One is kept breathless either by pleasure or by work."

Indeed things were becoming too hectic for Henrietta to safeguard even her precious Friday afternoon hours which she considered sacred to family letter-writing. On Wednesday she had traveled the forty-two miles to Tel Aviv for a very full day. Early Thursday morning she drove to Nahalat Yehudah to inspect the sand dunes to be leveled by the heads of 175 refugee families. These people were to be settled there in houses to be built on the sand. Henrietta was in a state of trepidation since she had to catch the ten o'clock bus to Ras-el-Ain. "Lo and behold! my auto stuck in the sand two feet deep, and it took fifteen minutes to dig out," she complained. "Then a dash to Ras-el-Ain, with the result that I sat on the hot railway platform there for two hours until the delayed train came up from Eqypt." The result was that the visit to Nahalat had to be made after nightfall. On Friday she had similar excitement, reaching Jerusalem only minutes before the Sabbath. "Well, at least the strike is over, and for that let us give praise and thanks." The Arab High Committee had called off the general strike on October 12, resulting in a precarious peace.

One pleasant episode in Henrietta's frenzied life occurred in mid-October when ground was broken on Mount Scopus for the Hadassah Nurses' Training School, the first of three buildings that would constitute the Hadassah Medical Center. One newspaper carried a photograph of her vigorously wielding a pick, along with the caption: "The founder of Hadassah breaks ground for the Medical Center in Palestine. Miss Szold, who started the welfare work of the organization twenty-five years ago, turns the first soil for a building to cost $850,000 on Mount Scopus near Jerusalem." Another photograph pictured Henrietta along with other dignitaries. Heading the speakers' list, which included her, were Dr. H. Yassky, director of the Hadassah Hospital; Dr. Judah L. Magnes, president of the Hebrew University; Daniel Auster, vice-Mayor of Jerusalem; and David Ben-Gurion, chairman of the Executive of the Jewish Agency for Palestine. The ceremony was held at eight-thirty in the morning, after which Henrietta had to rush off to Tel Aviv for the weekly meeting of the Refugee Camps Liquidating Committee.

From Haifa she wrote to Benjamin on November 2:

We are succeeding in breaking up the camps and transferring the refugees to homes in Tel Aviv and to some of the moshavim. But we are not solving their problems. In Nahalat Yehudah the 220 children of the 120 families settled there are roaming the streets of Rishon-le-Zion. There is no place for them in the schools. A number of the families are living in tents, and the rainy season is approaching. Their own houses, at the building of which they are to be employed, will not be completed for several months. Meanwhile individual problems are multiplying among the Youth Aliyah groups. They constitute my present mission in Haifa.

By mid-November Henrietta had finished her big job in Tel Aviv: all the refugee camps had been liquidated. A week later she returned from a four days' strenuous trip as far north as Tel Hai and to Kibbutz Kinneret on Lake Kinneret. A decrepit Egged bus from Afula, in the Jezreel Valley south of Nazareth, was so slow that she reached home minutes before the Sabbath.

Great Britain had appointed a Royal Commission to visit Palestine and gather evidence on the riots. The Commission, headed by William Robert Wellesley Peel, Viscount Clanfield, was also to suggest remedies for the chronic state of unrest. Benjamin Levin wrote to his brother on December 1:

The Royal Commission is here now hearing evidence. Dr. Weizmann gave them a lecture on elementary Zionism. Later Government officials testified as to their departments. The Arabs announced officially that they would boycott the Commission. Then they sent a representative to pay a "social call" on the members of the Commission and laid their demands before them "unofficially."

The old city of Jerusalem is still a danger spot. Right under the nose of the Royal Commission two Jews were wounded there by shots from ambushed Arabs.

The Spanish Civil War is looked upon everywhere as the preliminary bout of the coming world war.

The Vaad Leumi handed Henrietta the task of putting in order the material for its memoranda of grievances to be presented to the Royal Commission. An entire week of her time, day and night, had been swallowed up by this work. In addition she was to appear in person before the Royal Commission, and that, too required preparation.

Henrietta described for her family her seventy-sixth birthday on

December 21, 1936:

> It was a hectic day. Bouquets walked in all day long. And the next day some more, and some more, and now I am ruefully contemplating the piles of acknowledgments to be made. This time I have determined to be "efficient"—I have had cards printed. But who knows whether I'll get the time to address them. I was silly enough to try to work on the Royal Commission Memorandum on my birthday with all the excitement surging around me. The result was that I was a wreck the rest of the week. This morning, however, I finished the pesky thing.

Adele Seltzer's birthday greetings from Bridgeport arrived a bit late:

> A letter written in Connecticut on December 16 will not, alas, reach Jerusalem on December 21. But one cannot say that your birthday had not already occupied me. The Hadassahites, of course, have been planning, planning, planning. A playlet was to be composed which would be broadcast on your birthday. What's happening I don't know, because I've washed my hands of it. The broadcasting company will re-vamp the stuff—what do they know? Your sapient Emma, whom I met yesterday by chance at the Hadassah office and had dinner with, very wisely remarked that the Hadassah women each make of you a sublimation of themselves. That must be one of the elements that enters into myth-making. For I have seen a myth, a gigantic myth, grow up about you.

CHAPTER 4

JEWISH IMMIGRATION INTO PALESTINE CURTAILED; HITLER'S VICTIMS INCREASE

The Royal Commission conducted its investigations in Palestine until late January 1937, when it returned to England. Henrietta felt that even though the Commission's report proved to be moderate, attempting to appease both sides, the Arabs would continue their violence.

"Concerning myself there is the same old thing to report: submergence under waves of work, appearance on the surface only for the purpose of listening to every variety of tragic tale of hard luck and illness that go beyond the imagination of the Greek poets, and mental fatigue beyond description," Henrietta recorded on February 5, 1937. "This week there was one lucid interval; Max Schloessinger has been most generous to me, he takes me to all the Palestine Symphony Orchestra concerts. They transport me back to my girlhood when I never missed a Peabody Symphony concert in addition to the public rehearsal on the previous day."

Henrietta loved music. In the *Jerusalem Post Magazine* for March 11, 1983, Nahum "Tim" Gidal, a photographer who often traveled with her, recalled that as they drive along Henrietta would ask him to sing a song. Gidal had a good voice and was always happy to oblige.

Adele Seltzer wrote to Mrs. Felix Warburg on October 18, 1935: "When I was a child Henrietta, who was—can you believe it?—a brilliant performer on the piano, used to play me to sleep most nights in the week with Beethoven Sonatas." Henrietta was sixteen when Adele was born.

And Mrs. Hanna Marx, widow of Dr. Alexander Marx, historian at the Jewish Theological Seminary in New York, wrote to Bertha Levin in 1953: "A cherished memory for life will be the afternoons of one winter when your dear mother and sister came to us every fortnight and we read Browning together. At the end your sister and I played regularly from a volume of Beethoven's symphonies for four hands. How well she played!''

At Jerusalem the Fifth Annual Social Service Conference was soon to take place, and on the last evening Henrietta expected to launch her long-cherished plan of coordinating all the child and youth agencies. ''I am more than a little doubtful if it will be accepted,'' she wrote on February 5. ''However there is one gain, I'll have got it out of my system where it has been incubating many years.''

Throughout March, April and May Henrietta was a ''wandering Jewess,'' visiting youth groups at various settlements where she saw the children in all stages of development from six months of age on up. That summer Henrietta sailed for the Zionist Congress in Zürich. En route to Trieste she wrote on July 23:

> Today's Bulletin from London as to the procedure suggested in the Commons with reference to the discussion of the Royal Commission Report is most satisfactory I think. At least it gives assurance of serious consideration of a serious subject. I doubt whether in the end it will bring the sort of solution I dream of—conciliation between Arab and Jew in Palestine. At least we shall not be hurried into an ill-considered action.

The Royal Commission had recommended that the Mandated territory should be divided into three parts—a Jewish state, an Arab state including Trans-Jordan, and a British mandated zone along the railroad from Jaffa to Jerusalem. The World Zionist Congress in Zürich favored the plan with certain changes, but the Pan-Arab Congress voted against it. Nothing ever came of the project.

From Zürich Henrietta traveled to Berlin, chiefly to talk to the parents of the large contingent of boys and girls who were soon to leave for Emek Ha-Yarden, a colony in the Jezreel Valley. Although the parents were ''living corpses'' with no hope of saving themselves, their one thought was for their children's safety. The experience was a great emotional strain for Henrietta who then returned to Zürich for the Second Biennial Conference of the Youth Immigration.

In early October Henrietta embarked for the United States on the Cunard White Star *Georgic*. The passage was a comfortable one with scarcely a wave on the Atlantic. But she was disturbed by some of the bulletins from Jerusalem. Apparently terrorism was again prevalent, as bad as anything that had occurred since April 1936, the beginning of the excitement. The murder of Avinoam Yellin, son of David Yellin, professor of Hebrew poetry at the Hebrew University, was particularly distressing to her. The thirty-seven-year-old educator and orientalist had been killed by Arab rioters.

Henrietta had agreed to attend the Hadassah Convention to report on Youth Aliyah. But she had made them promise not to make her the center of publicity. She wrote to Benjamin and his wife from Bertha Levin's home in Baltimore on December 5:

> I have been catapulted from person to person, from place to place, from subject to subject in so hectic a fashion that some duties and some pleasures had to suffer. Aunt Adele stayed with me in New York the two days between my arrival and my going to Atlantic City for the Hadassah Convention which was an imposing demonstration. It lasted for a week.

Henrietta found Hadassah to be "a marvelous, flexible, well-oiled machine." The convention had voted $25,000 as a memorial to Felix M. Warburg, the Jewish communal leader and philanthropist who had fought vigorously against restrictions on Jewish immigration to Palestine imposed by the British Mandatory Government. This money was to be incorporated into Henrietta's Children's Central Fund. In addition Hadassah was giving her a birthday present of $5,000 for the placement of children. She felt it had been worth coming so far to receive such gifts and so much affection.

From Atlantic City she headed for "Sweet Cicily," Adele's place in Easton. "We drove around the Connecticut roads in all directions, and I feasted my eyes on the country of the temperate zone; even though there was no foliage left, there were the gracious vistas I love," Henrietta told Benjamin. When she and Adele were not exploring the countryside, Henrietta browsed in Adele's barn where Henrietta's household goods were stored. She read over old letters and disposed of some of her furniture and other possessions which it was a pity to leave unused. Then on to Baltimore where she found that the family had become numerous: "There is constant coming and going, and dashing around in Chevrolets." Adele added a note to Henrietta's letter: "We're having a positively tumultuous life; a dozen rings to the circus going at once. And I enjoy the various homes—your mother's, Harriet's, Sarah's, Jas's. We had a lovely walk this afternoon along Gwynns Falls."

Henrietta's splendid seventy-eighth birthday celebration was over.

It was hard for her to say goodbye to Bertha, Adele, and the rest of the family. She wrote to Benjamin from on board the S.S. *Manhattan* on January 10, 1938:

> Altogether the parting was hard, harder than ever before, at least for me. I suppose my depression in the matter of our political situation reflects itself in personal affairs too. I cannot understand the Zionists who are rejoicing over the prospect of a statelet to be launched at a time of international conflicts and menace. The outlook is particularly dark in the Mediterranean basin. I suppose the young must be depended upon to meet this emergency.
>
> I am within a few hours of Plymouth where I am to disembark for a two weeks' stay in England. That brings me to Palestine at the end of January. This Atlantic passage was the worst I have ever experienced. A heavy sea bore down upon us, and these last three days have been a constant movie show, with crashing dishes, dancing chairs, sliding tables, and falling passengers. I was among the last. Big, mountainous waves dashed me down twice. I got off with bruises, but it might have been bad, as it was for others who broke ribs. One poor sailor was swept overboard. He could not be rescued, nor was his body recovered.

After running into Haifa harbor aboard the S.S. *Galilea,* Henrietta was quickly back in harness. She wrote from Jerusalem on February 20 that she was about to start out on a three days' tour to Haifa and its surroundings. A group of German boys had to be met at the port and taken to Mikve Israel, the first agricultural school to be founded in the country. After escorting the boys to Mikve Israel Henrietta planned to spend that night in Tel Aviv at Moskowitz's on Hayarkon Street near Trumpeldor. She always stayed at that pension where the Hungarian cooking reminded her of her mother's. A couple of weeks later she stopped off again at Mikve Israel to see how the twenty-five German boys were getting along. They were a group of religious youths who had been assigned a dormitory and a dining room of their own, along with two Madrichim, or counselors, of their own. This was an interesting experiment and apparently promised success.

That March of 1938 German troops occupied Austria. Henrietta wrote on the 18th:

> Good Purim! I cannot say that my feelings are festive. Perhaps, nevertheless, they are in accord with the spirit of Haman's and

Amalek's evaluation in Jewish tradition. I can't think of anything but Hitler's hellish efficiency in the matter of Austria. As a matter of fact, I am depressed by what has happened, not first and foremost by reason of the fate of the Jews, but by what it forebodes for humanity. Is it possible to avoid the bloodiest war of history after what this week brought the world? And Czechoslovakia cannot but be the next victim. The whole world stands glaring at Germany, and not one power can raise a finger in protest or for help.

We have already begun discussing preparations for the incorporation of the Austria-German boys and girls in our Youth Aliyah rescue work. Fortunately the certificates situation in the new immigration regulations is most auspicious. Students' certificates, the category of the Youth Aliyah, are unlimited. Of course, for us there is a limitation to their use—money on the one side and the number of available places in the country on the other. The Jewish world has had so many shocks that one wonders whether even such a catastrophe as that of the Austrian Jews will evoke a response in terms of money. As for places, we have already mobilized 1200. As you see, there is work ahead.

By the first week in April Henrietta had received three postcards from her Viennese relatives. Not one conveyed anything but a "Lebenszeichen"—a sign of life. Obviously they did not dare go into particulars. Henrietta had heard reports of a few Austrian Jews who had managed to escape from Hitler's Viennese hell to Palestine. "What the Germans learnt in the Reich in the course of five years they have applied with Satanic efficiency in Vienna in the course of as many days," she commented. "I have been told by a Palestinian just returned from Europe, where he visited a number of places, that everywhere the Jews 'sit in darkness' wondering what will be their fate; and the others are ready to embrace Hitler-Napoleon when he comes, as they think he is bound to come." Henrietta could not bring herself to think of anything else. One bright spot in the darkness was a cable from Hadassah: Eddie Cantor had collected $32,000 for the Austrian Youth Aliyah.

Henrietta wrote from the Hotel Eden on May 6:

The Austrian situation is overwhelming me. Practically daily I get a letter from one of our relatives in Vienna—some of them want certificates, some inquire whether I can secure affidavits for them for America. And the Youth Immigration movement authorities are besieged by Austria, Germany, Roumania, Poland, and even Czechoslovakia. Palestine in the grip of guerrilla warfare is still looked upon as a haven of refuge for the hounded Jews of Central Europe.

She wrote again on June 3:

> According to today's paper 1200 boys and girls have registered in Vienna for the Youth Aliyah. We shall be lucky if we can bring 400 over. In Vienna the organization of such an undertaking will be much more difficult than it was in Germany. The Austrians were never famous for system and order, and the Jews have no means. It was intended that I go to Vienna for the purpose. But the Gestapo thought otherwise. It specifically forbade my coming, on pain of trouble to the home people. It mentioned me by name! The thoroughness of the Nazis is hellish.
>
> The one personal lesson I have derived is that I am not, perhaps never have been, a pacifist. I want Germany to be chastened, and there is no chastisement but war.

In mid-July a report reached Henrietta that a bomb had exploded in the vegetable market of Jerusalem's Old City. It was said that scores had been killed and wounded. Among those killed were at least ten of the poor Arab peasant women who came there to market their pitiful produce. Would the outrage be laid at the door of the Jews? "The events of the week are too ghastly to write about," Henrietta complained on July 29. "I am suffering in particular because my most knowing friends are of the firm opinion that the bomb-makers and throwers are Jews. If that is true, something subversive is going to happen to my Zionism."

"Today my mind is so full of the Italian racialism which, the papers say, will presently affect 10,000 Jews, who must leave Italy within six months, that I can't write about anything else," Henrietta told Benjamin on September 2. "That is one of my grudges against Hitler, that his venom keeps one from dwelling on any phase of life except that which he has infected." She found it soothing to read her sister Bertha's leters. Bertha's two young grandchildren, Betsy Levin and Louis Terrell, engaged her attention. Henrietta envied Bertha: "She has two little lightning rods by her side—they keep her serene."

Henrietta's exhausting schedule landed her in the hospital, under treatment for a tired heart. When she wrote again on October 4, she was feeling improved although her full working powers had not yet returned. "Did you see in the morning's paper that all sections of American Jewry—warring upon each other until recently— are taking united action with reference to the political lot of Palestine? One thing seems almost certain—Partition is dead."

Despite her tired heart, Henrietta plunged ahead with her work. On November 19 she had a cable from London, from the executive members of the Vaad Leumi, the National Council of the Jews in Palestine, who had gone there for the sessions of the Vaad Ha-Poel, the Executive Council of Labor. The Executive announced on behalf of the Vaad Leumi that it would bring 5000 children from Germany. "I am sure they don't know that to execute such a plan requires $500,000, for transfer of the candidates and their support and schooling for a year," she lamented. "Besides there is the question of certificates! It's like the story of the Pied Piper of Hamelin reversed—the children are the pipes."

Bertha had written of the birth of her third grandchild, Larry. Henrietta wrote to the proud parents, Jastrow and Zan:

> My congratulations and my warmest welcome to Lawrence Lee Levin—what a liquid alliteration!...I haven't anything half so interesting to report as the coming of Lawrence to town. To be sure, I, too, am thinking about children, but not one; my concern is five thousand, or ten thousand, with a few thousand adolescents thrown in for good measure. From a father's and mother's point of view I fancy five thousand are not equal to even half a child. Yet, I want to assure you, they, the five thousand, are a great responsibility, especially as we can't wrap them in a blanket and keep them snug and warm, since certificates are refused them by the great British Empire. It's a devastating state of affairs. I suppose you are both too modern to add a bug-a-boo to your pedagogic paraphernalia. In strictest confidence I want to tell you that of all the bug-a-boos that ever existed in fairyland or unintellectual nurseries, Hitler is the greatest of them all.

With around 400,000 Jews in Palestine, together with about 900,000 Moslems and 100,000 Christians, mostly Arab, the British issued the White Paper of 1939 announcing their intention to create a single independent state predominantly Arab in population. This state paper also provided for limiting Jewish immigration to 1,500 persons a month and for cutting it off entirely in 1944, when the Jewish population was expected to reach 500,000.

Henrietta wrote to her sisters, Bertha and Adele, on March 3:

It has been a bleak week-constant rain and unmitigated depression among the Jews. Only the most optimistic among the incorrigible optimists have clung to a shred of hope. What is happening in London is not really a surprise, but it is as little intelligible as Munich. From the international point of view nothing suffices to justify or explain it. If Britain stood by for twenty years while Jews poured in substance, and work, and built in an unprecedented manner, and paid the bills of the British and the Arabs, there was only one thing for Britain to do—risk Arab disloyalty and treachery in the eventuality of war. If Britain held back from giving security to the Jews, but allowed them to be harried and murdered and pillaged, and admired their self-restraint, at least ostensibly, these three years, she had no right to invite as her chief advisers and as petted guests the instigators of the crimes. Everybody, of course, goes on with his business as though the bottom had not dropped out. But I am sure one question is pounding in everyone's head: on what foundation shall I be standing tomorrow?

And at this moment of supreme agony, when the new dispersion is taking place, and threatens to grow until it extends over Continental Europe, the little refuge built with unparalleled sacrifices may not take in the refugees. The bitter irony of our lot is that on the day on which 360,000 Jews are added to the Hitler victims, the only door of hope which might have been held open is slammed in our faces.

Although from the beginning of the London Conferences it was foreseen that the Jews were to be the victims, Henrietta had not been prepared for the naked cynicism of the proceedings and the proposals. She was disturbed that she had been unable to secure certificates for any of her trapped Szold relatives in Europe. Yet in spite of her solemn thoughts, Henrietta hoped that the wedding of Bertha's youngest child, Eva Leah, would go off happily.

Bertha Szold Levin and Adele
Szold Seltzer visited their
sister, Henrietta in Palestine in
1939.

Viola Yellin, Judith
Yellin, Yona Yellin,
Adele Seltzer holding
Bushy the cat,
Jerusalem, 1939.
Henrietta became
very fond of the cat.

Henrietta Szold at the Hebrew University Library Building on the occasion of the transfer there of her father's manuscripts of his *Commentary on the Book of Job*, 1941. Her secretary, Emma Ehrlich, is third from the left. Dr. Judah L. Magnes is behind and to left of Henrietta.

Wendell Willkie calling on Henrietta Szold, 1942, Jerusalem.

CHAPTER 5

THE THREE SISTERS

In March 1939 Henrietta's sisters, Bertha Levin and Adele Seltzer, sailed aboard the *Ile de France* to visit her in Palestine. Bertha was a widow, but childless Adele had left her husband Thomas to fend for himself in Connecticut. Thomas Seltzer, a small publisher, had brought out more D.H. Lawrence first editions than any other American publisher before or since. But Thomas was a poor businessman, and after his firm's collapse it was taken over by his nephews, the Boni brothers. The Seltzers, in relatively straightened circumstances, struggled to ride out the Great Depression.

From aboard the *Ile de France* Adele wrote to Thomas on March 24:

> Yesterday held unusual interest and flashed a bit of brilliance upon the dullness of shipboard life. The amusement began with a dispute at lunch, on one side the long-bearded rabbi from Mir, Poland, and on the other side two Belgians and the beautiful Parisienne. The rebbe finds the Mizrachi not pious enough. He goes under the tag of some other group, the name of which I did not catch. He is returning to Poland having been in the U.S.A. to raise money for a Yeshiva in Mir. The Belgian brothers were shaven, but wore skull caps and murmured a bit of Hebrew at table. In appearance you couldn't distinguish them from a thousand successful American Jewish businessmen. The steamer is due to arrive at Havre at 6:30 P.M. *after* Shabbas. Horrors! *After* Shabbas. The rebbe said that several policemen would have to drag him from the boat where he proposed to stay the whole of Friday night and the whole of Shabbas. The steamship line told him they would insist upon his leaving. He doesn't sit at *our* Kosher table, but came to us (with a bottle of

33

wine filched from his table tucked under his gabardine) to tell us his story. The more talkative of the two Belgian brothers told him that if he was so pious he ought not to eat even at the Kosher table, but only food prepared by himself on dishes washed by himself. The rebbe retorted that the Belgian was an anti-Semite and an Am ha-Aretz. The Parisenne landed on him in a voluable stream of Yiddish, defending the Belgians, saying that men who wore caps and ate at a Kosher table were *not* anti-Semites. The Belgian said scathingly that rebbes who tucked wine bottles under their gabardines were a shame to the race, and a rebbe who wanted to preserve influence over the youths in his Yeshiva had better not, *nowhere* in the world, call young men Am ha-Aretzim. The Parisienne added that before taking the boat he should have ascertained the time of arrival, and taken a swifter (and more expensive) boat that made the trip between two Shabbases. She then told of her father, an Austrian rabbi, a well-known one by the name of Fränkel, *ein so feiner und güter mensch,* that he gave away everything he owned and kept nothing for himself. Once on a trip that he had to undertake suddenly to save his sick wife, he had eaten nothing but eggs boiled by himself. *That* was piety, she said. She couldn't see that the Mir rebbe made sacrifices for his piety. He only put others, in this case the French line, to trouble.

Later I asked the rebbe why he had called the Belgian an Am ha-Aretz. "Weil, er *ist* ein Am ha-Aretz," he said. Bertha and I had to laugh, of course. Still later, the mashgi'ah came to me on deck while I was reading to ask what the violent talk at table had been about. Was the food criticized? He had caught something about eggs and sufficiently kosher plates. My report of the conversation soothed him. Then *he* let loose about the rebbe. The rebbe was travelling with a mythical sum of money, thousands of dollars, perhaps $40,000, perhaps $50,000. "But he collected that for the Yeshiva," I said. "Er *ist* der Yeshiva," said the mashgi'ah. I had to laugh again. But really, you know how I agonize over such revelations of mediaevalism.

Bertha and Adele reached Palestine on Monday, April 5. Five days later Bejamin Levin wrote from Kfar Syrkin to his sister, Mrs. Harriet Terrell at Baltimore:

Of course the exciting event of the past week was meeting Mamma and Aunt Adele. At the last minute we learned that the *D'Artagnan* would dock at Tel Aviv and we went there Monday morning. Sarah and I had never been to the port before and for some time we wandered about the grounds of the adjacent Levant Fair before we found the right entrance. Finally we reached the dock and through the gates we could see Aunt Henrietta and Emma Ehrlich. The gateman did not want to let us through but fortunately I had some visiting cards with me, one of which I sent in to Aunt Henrietta. Immediately we had the gates opened for us. We found that we had arrived in the nick of time, for at that moment a motorboat was bringing Mamma and Aunt Adele to the dock. Chaim Weizmann had been travelling on the same ship but had come ashore a few minutes before and we missed him.

All along on the trip up to Jerusalem one of the striking things was the way in which Aunt Adele was impressed by what she saw. Tel Aviv in particular was a pleasant disappointment to her. She had been told that it was an ugly city, and she found it "jolly."

It took Adele a few days at the Hotel Eden before her first impressions solidified sufficiently for her to write to husband Thomas on April 7:

I am already prepared to say that the building of the Jewish Homeland is a remarkable, a fascinating, a thrilling adventure, perhaps even a glorious undertaking. But—my "but" is greater than ever. Along with the upbuilding goes also the upbuilding in a magnified degree of national ego, harmless enough, I suppose, for the Jews alone, but awful in its general effect where the same national egotism affects nation upon nation. If it weren't that what the Jews have done here is so interesting, the chauvenism would drive me straight back to our retreat in Easton.

Adele told Thomas that so far as sightseeing was concerned, there was little one could do. She had been shown a part of the Wailing Wall, but the very heart of the Old City, where the Arab bazaars were, was barred to all outsiders. Armored cars patroled the streets, and Jewish, Arab and English guards were everywhere. There were barricades along most of the roads leading into the city, along with curfew and searches for arms. Even non-prohibited spots were unsafe. The curator of the Rockefeller Museum, an Englishman, had been shot as he was putting his car into his garage in a supposedly safe section of the city. Adele's letter concluded:

The Arabs have, for the moment, concentrated their killings upon the English and their own countrymen who decently refuse to play with the gangsters. I just received a letter concluding: "Hope you keep well and don't get shot"—a comic commentary on the times. Another funny one I heard: A man preceded a statement with: "If peace should break out."

Bertha Levin wrote home to her family on April 19, that she, Adele, and Mrs. Mordecai M. Kaplan, wife of the founder of the Reconstructionist movement in the United States, had been at Natanya, a lovely seaside resort. They were joined there by Henrietta and Hans Beyth who had met a Youth Aliyah group disembarking at Tel Aviv. Bertha described the trip:

> After lunch we piled into the car and drove away from that indescribably beautiful spot not without its alarums, illegal immigrants, etc. On our way to Haifa we stopped at an institution in which there are children from Germany. While Henrietta and Mr. Beyth conferred with the head, we three tourists were led around the place by a charming boy who had spent some time in England. Though he left Germany at the age of 9, if you asked him anything about the country, he said, "I have forgotten."
>
> Yesterday we had a big tour in the part of the Emek near Haifa. We saw the kvutzoth of the first "graduates" of the Youth Aliyah, another home for children from Germany, and finally, in the outskirts of Haifa, a perfect home for the purpose called Ahava, as fine as any such institution anywhere. After dinner we dropped into bed dead tired. When one goes with Henrietta one starts at 7 A.M. with breakfast and goes on till 6 P.M. or later.

Bertha wrote home again from Tel Aviv's Pension Moscowitz on April 25:

> Yesterday Adele and I went to the Histadrut Office Building to see Goldie Meyerson. She was in Jerusalem, but a Mrs. Kaplan took us in tow and Adele had a long interview with her on the subject of the women's branch of the work. This morning by appointment we returned to Mrs. Kaplan's office and she showed us several institutions. Among them was a center for training immigrants, a weaving establishment, the WIZO baby home for triplets, twins, premature infants and some social case babies, and a *meshek* for training girls in farm work, a lovely place. They have 22 dunams for 80 girls, 25

cows, and hundreds of chickens. Every inch is intensively cultivated, and the produce sold sustains the establishment. Being
Geverat Szold's sisters we were presented with beautiful bouquets
of roses.

In Palestine everyone addressed Henrietta in the third person. She
was always "Geveret" Szold—"Miss" Szold, "our" Miss Szold.

In Jerusalem the three sisters enjoyed the company of their first
cousin, Miriam Schaar Schloessinger, and her husband Max. Miriam
had amassed a fascinating collection of antique lamps, a curiosity of
which were several lamps of the ancient Jewish period decorated with
swastikas. Adele wrote to Thomas on May 1 about a four-day visit to
Natanya, "the Jewish Riviera," where the Max Schloessingers had a
summer cottage:

> While there we were driven to orange groves and to an interesting
> farm beyond a Jewish village, Hadera. At Kfar Syrkin we had a good
> opportunity to see the relation existing between the common British
> soldiers and the Jews. An excellent one. A very, very bad one be-
> tween the soldiers and the Arabs.
>
> We have been back in Jerusalem two days after a trip to Rehovot
> where Weizmann lives and works in the Sieff chemical laboratory
> and agricultural experiment station. I know all about the ways
> thousands of illegals are sneaked into the country. Strange to say,
> Henrietta approves of their entering *sub rosa*. We saw the British
> soliders search an Arab village for arms and ammunition. One is
> fairly safe if one does not venture into exclusively Arab sections.
> However around some of the collectives Arabs set land mines at
> night, and to step on them may or may not mean death.

The next day the sisters breakfasted at 6:45, then were off in a taxi with
Hans Beyth. Bertha and Adele were impressed by the "overwhelming" beauty of Nazareth, Cana, and Tiberias on the Sea of Galilee. The
afternoon was spent at Rosh Pinah where they saw a group of twenty
Youth Aliyah children. The handsome set of boys and girls, many from
Vienna, had been in the country only a month. Henrietta, Mr. Beyth,
and a Miss Jabotinsky, sister of Vladimir Jabotinsky, discussed hotly
and at great length with two men concerning changing the children's
housing arrangements. Later the sisters saw the children in a
classroom learning Hebrew. At the end of the lesson Henrietta spoke
to them in German.

Several days after their return to Jerusalem, Bertha and Adele visited Bethlehem and the pools were Solomon sent his many wives to bathe. The disturbances had taken a serious turn there as evidenced by the shattered, smoke-blackened ruins.

The three sisters were off again on one of their flying tours. On the way from Jerusalem to Tel Aviv they visited several colonies and saw Chaim Weizmann's "lordly" estate at Rehovot. Adele wrote to Thomas from Tel Aviv's Pension Moscowitz on May 13:

> Today I had a most interesting conversation with Goldie Meyerson, a chief propagandist in the Histadrut. In a few days I will be ready to write my article on Palestine. Title: "The Great Will." Angle of approach: the noble structure that England is destroying. I have asked several of the more intelligent labor people here: "Supposing Palestine had been nothing but an aggregate of orange-growing colonies such as existed before the Balfour Declaration, what would England's attitude have been?" The answer was: "The opposite of what it has been." It is quite apparent that England has *not*, as we supposed, been afraid of an Arab national movement. She has simply supported the rich class the Arab leaders in their personal claims. Plutocrat allying with plutocrat.

CHAPTER 6

THE WHITE PAPER
INCREASES THE TERRORISM

On May 17, 1939, the MacDonald White Paper was issued by the British. It announced that the government would "regard it as contrary to their obligations to the Arabs under the Mandate, as well as to the assurances which had been given to the Arab people in the past, that the Arab population of Palestine should be made the subjects of a Jewish State against their will."* It further stated that it desired to see the creation of an independent state in which both Jews and Arabs would share authority in government so that the essential interests of each would be secured. The Jewish Agency protested, charging that the British government intended to set up a territorial ghetto for the Jews in their own homeland. Jewish demonstrations in Palestine against the White Paper degenerated into serious riots.

From the Hotel Eden Bertha Levin wrote to her daughter, Harriet Terrell, on May 19:

> Yesterday's strike and demonstrations seem to have passed off smoothly till darkness fell and then the people got out of hand and imitated the hoodlum methods of the *goyim*. Too bad! For the Jews are so in the right and the British so in the wrong. Somehow or other the Jews must hold on to what they have done and develop it.
>
> We three spent the day quietly in the hotel, though it seems the big parade that was staged was worth seeing since it had all types and ages of Jews in it, the orientals dressed in their gay costumes

---

*Paul L. Hanna, British Policy in Palestine (Wash., D.C.: American Council on Public Affairs, 1942), 147-149.

and the schoolboys in their blue and khaki uniforms. We got news of the parade and meetings from the callers we had almost all day. Henrietta likes strikes because they give her a chance to answer the letters that pile up from Youth Aliyah childrens' parents, and our relations. She is swamped by that correspondence, and worried by the problems that arise in the Youth Aliyah groups, boys that run away, etc. The situation has in these five years grown more complicated, not only because Vienna, Czechoslovakia, etc. have been added to Germany, but because parents had arrived here and the matter of visits from the young people crops up. Traveling through the country was forbidden the youths by Henrietta on account of the highly dangerous conditions since '36.

In America it was announced over the radio that a number of women had demonstrated in Jerusalem with an American woman, aged seventy-eight, at their head. A number of Hadassah women and Thomas Seltzer jumped to the conclusion that the woman was Henrietta. Thomas marveled at what a change had come over the world if his rather proper sister-in-law led a demonstration. Adele corrected the assumption on June 9:

> No, Henrietta did *not* take part in the demonstration. The lady of 78 was a Mrs. Yellin. Henrietta felt that she could not endanger her good reputation with the British on account of the Youth Aliyah. The British might retaliate by depriving her of the entry certificates for her young people. Oddly enough, during the demonstration she was fast asleep, worn out by all the agitation that preceded it. Though it was her office hours, Bertha and I managed to keep secretaries away until she woke up naturally.

Bertha recorded in her diary for Friday, May 26: "6 A.M. Explosion that wrecked telephone." On June 14 Adele wrote to Thomas in Connecticut:

> Even before the White Paper was issued, when it was just threatening, Henrietta said to us that she was afraid the Jewish hotheads would resort to violence, and that some plan other than a plan of violence should be promoted by the Jewish authorities. I asked her if she had anything to suggest. She said that to her mind the only thing that occurred was for the Jews not to import, in order not to pay so much in taxes to the Government, and to satisfy themselves

with whatever the country itself produced.

I asked her whether she realized that in order to enforce such a measure the Jews would have to have a totalitarian government to themselves. As a matter of fact, the super-patriots now by orders from above are poking into people's iceboxes to see if the eggs inside are native-born. Now economic conditions here on account of the Arab terror and the baleful mixing in of the British are awful. The situation here intensifies the depression everywhere existing. Just to give you a small notion of how it works. Cinemas are closed. People are afraid to go to a hotel for dances and that sort of thing. There are no tourists. The shops are dead. In such circumstances, when people are so desperately poor, they will continue to buy Syrian eggs which are half the price of Palestinian eggs because the production cost of them is cheaper. Spying and denunciation have already begun.

The Jews have a terror of their own now. Merry accompaniment to the Arab terror. What do Jews want with terror? What do they need more than the few bombs and sticks of dynamite that blow up the inside of the postoffice? They need an army and navy and air force. Where will they get it?

Adele was upset by what she saw of the internal factionalism of the Palestinian Jews. She explained to Thomas on June 18:

They are frightfully divided among themselves, fairly hating one another. The Histadrut got the Government to banish Jabotinsky, the Revisionist, but now is itself going totalitarian, not under its former leader Weizmann, but under Ben Gurion. Weizmann has lost out: the charge is, he's too pro-English. Maybe he has been pro-English. But if he hadn't been, then the charge would have been that he offended the English.

The upbuilding of this country had been miraculous. So, too, the change it has wrought in the physique, not in one generation, but in less than a generation. A shabby sort of a creature develops over-night into a demi-god—not in the cities, just in the collectives. They are the handsomest men I have ever seen.

Adele had been a guest at a young people's party where the attractive hostess was an expert photographer who did all the work for the Hebrew University's archeological department. Another guest was a young English army officer. The rest were German couples. It was a gay affair until there came over the radio the news that Danzig had gone over to Germany. The news proved to be false next day, but upon hearing it at the party the Englishman burst out that it surely meant war, that Chamberlain would have to let it mean war. Adele's letter to Thomas continued:

> The English, it seems to me, are getting to be a bit ashamed of England. He said England ought not to make promises she can't keep—meaning the promise to help the Jews with their Homeland.
>
> Speaking of the English—their Tommies are a frightfully homely species. In spite of the bronzing done by the scorching Palestinian sun, they give the impression of being pasty-faced. Their figures are lanky, but ungraceful and by no means suggesting power. Their features are negative, their expression blank. However, they have without exception, drawing-room manners, and that goes a long way. The Jews, alas, are not so impolite as a bit uncouth, lacking polish. But get into conversation with them, and you ask for nothing more than the intrinsic courtesy that all fine people possess. The young Germans at the photographer's party had excellent manners. Yet they, too, lack the final finish of the English. So do I. For looks, give me the handsome young Jews.
>
> The persons I feel most comfortable with are the unprejudiced young, though even these are prickly with their nationalism. Nevertheless you can let your thoughts go more freely with them. With the others, the older people, including my two sisters, I feel like a naughty school child.
>
> If a spool of thread is produced in Palestine, it's not an ordinary spool of thread. It is a sanctified spool of thread. It is a Jewish-national spool of thread. It is a cultural spool of thread. Darn with it, and you darn into the hole in your stocking a "way of life," a Judeo-cultural way of life, a Mosaic, an Isaiahic way of life, a peculiarly ethical way of life. At the moment I happen to be engulfed in the atmosphere of magnified nationalism, and I can't help expressing how it affects me. It's a good thing that the thousands of hens in Palestine don't feel the way I do. If they did, and if they realized that each egg they laid was considered to be the result, not so much of a sexual as of a Jewish cultural process, they might stop laying eggs.

Two days later Adele entered Dr. Stern's sanitorium for treatment of intestinal troubles she was experiencing. She was soon better but not completely recovered.

On Wednesday, June 28, Henrietta and her sisters moved from the Eden Hotel to a furnished first floor apartment at Giacomon House, on King George Avenue. The idea for the apartment, rented from Henrietta's friends, Dr. and Mrs. Klinger, was that at the Eden she had only one room, with running water but no private bath. Since by the doctor's orders Henrietta could not walk to the Hadassah office and she hesitated to spend money on a taxi, her one room served as bedroom, parlor, and office. People who came to see her on business often sat on her couch. Once she had had an invasion of bedbugs. But moving meant relinquishing a number of amenities. The hotel's cooking was exquisite, and when one was out, messages were intelligently taken. The proprietor nearly wept when Henrietta told him she was leaving. Must she go? Since the terror, tourist trade had fallen off. In the hotel with its forty rooms, large foyers, and dining room there were only the three sisters, a couple, a single lady, and a very occasional tourist.

King George Avenue, the sisters' new location, curved away from the main business street, the Jaffa Road, on its upward ascent. It was a fine residential street on the edge of two districts, Talbieh and Rechavia, which were like suburban developments. Opposite to their apartment was a large building with a walled garden, the Terra Sancta, an Italian mission school. On either side of them were large vacant lots with olive trees where flocks of goats with Arab herdsmen tried to eke some sustenance from the parched vegetation. Near them, on Julian's Way, which ran in a grand sweep into King George Avenue, was the imposing Y.M.C.A. building, an immense institution with a large central edifice and two great wings in an expanse of well-kept grounds. The apartment was near most of their friends. In an upstairs apartment lived the Yellins. Miriam and Max Schloessinger were but three minutes' walk away, as were Louis and Emma Ehrlich. Mr. Viteles, who kindly lent the sisters interesting books, lived opposite the Schloessingers. On the way to these friends one passed two veritable palaces belonging to the two richest Jews in Palestine, one of whom was a multi-millionaire.

"Yesterday's callers made the impression of a full-sized reception," Bertha wrote home from the apartment on July 23. "Adele always presides over the teacups but was caught too soon after her nap to be ready." Bertha had not dared leave the parlor full of people to be handled by Henrietta alone, especially as they were a conglomerate lot. Among the guests were an American missionary from Iowa and his Canadian wife, an elderly Scotswoman, and Dorothy Kahn, an

American social worker.

Bertha had assumed charge of the apartment's kitchen and was having trouble with the stove. ''Fire in kitchen—oil stove went up!'' she jotted in her diary for Tuesday, August 1. ''House a mess.'' Bertha, a plump sixty-six-year-old, had had to run excitedly to give the alarm at the Fire Department. On August 11 Adele notified Thomas:

> Two days ago Bertha collapsed from a heart attack. There's a day nurse, a night nurse, also a young Viennese physician on duty during the night for the steady administration of oxygen. Like all first heart attacks it came suddenly and unexpectedly. The housekeeping job, of course, falls on me. I did not undertake a trip to the Orient to bother with kosher meals, or any meals, for that matter. At best keeping house for Henrietta is not simple.
>
> The paper here is carrying worse and worse news, both about the sufferings of the ''illegal'' Jews and the terror in the land. The terror since the Jews have taken part in it on account of their resentment of the White Paper is somehow more sinister. It strikes the wrong people. Why plant bombs where persons with whom your sympathies are may be the same ones killed?

Adele wrote again to Thomas on August 15:

> This is the day I was to leave Palestine, and on this day we learned from the doctor that there will be no question of Bertha's leaving bed for another six weeks. Even after that she will have to be guarded carefully and allowed complete rest. That means I am doomed to housekeeping here for a long, long time. I'm hideously homesick.
>
> Henrietta is a dear. She's a darling. So unruffled now, so mellow. No acerbity, no censoriousness. Here's a funny story. Henrietta and I went to the Hadassah Hospital yesterday, and the superintendent, Dr. Yassky, begged Henrietta to go take a look at the babies. She was put into a large, sterilized white gown and led to where the day-old infants were ranged. While she was in there, the head nurse, a close friend of hers, came running. She had heard that Henrietta was in the obstetrical ward and came to see if the Messiah was being born!

CHAPTER 7

DESPITE PERSONAL SORROW, HENRIETTA CARRIES ON

Henrietta had expected to attend the Youth Aliyah Conference in Amsterdam but was forced to change her plans. Adele explained to Thomas on August 25, 1939:

> I am writing this on the third day after the stunning news reached us of the German-Russian pact. I am wondering what the Communists are finding to say by way of explanation and excuse. Russia clearly used Germany's necessity and England's unreliability to secure herself. Of course, by doing so, she strengthens Germany.
>
> Two days ago Henrietta was just about to leave for Amsterdam. In half an hour Mr. Beyth was to call for her in a taxi to drive to Haifa where they were to take the steamer, when a telegram came from Geneva telling her, but not explicitly, that she had better not embark. She sent a reply telegram that she was proceeding to Haifa, and they should wire her there again definitely whether or not she should come. At six o'clock in the evening she long-distanced me from Haifa that she was advised not to come, that a decision had been reached not to hold the conference in Amsterdam. She is not back, however, as she used the opportunity to visit some of the colonies in the Haifa district on behalf of the Youth Aliyah.
>
> Frankly life is dull, exceedingly dull. What with curfew and the general atmosphere of depression, Jerusalem is drab. You'd hardly conceive how at every minute I have America in mind, the country, the people, the life. Correspondence is getting expensive, isn't it? But I can't help using the *Yankee Clipper*. I'm getting nationalistic. I like to say "Yankee Clipper." It's got such a smart, cocky American ring.

Bertha's illness, after the first few days of terrible anxiety, had had a relaxing effect upon Henrietta. "It is really excellent for Henrietta to abandon her desk every now and then, between secretaries and callers, and run to Bertha's room for a light chat," Adele assured Bertha's family at home. "Bertha so amuses her, and as Bertha lies cheerfully in bed, getting the ministrations that one thinks came only to royalty and millionaires, one forgets that she is a patient and just has fun."

Meanwhile Henrietta had achieved an unexpected form of recognition. Benjamin had once told her that she had not reached the pinnacle of fame because her likeness had not appeared on a sardine box. "Well, you have surpassed that," he wrote from Kfar Syrkin on September 4. "The other day Sarah found a child playing with a picture card from a cigarette package with your photo on it! The cigarette boxes now carry picture cards of the Famous Men and Women series!"

Life took a more serious turn that September of 1939. "At this writing, all we know is that German troops have gone into Poland, and German air raids on Polish cities have been made," Adele informed Thomas on the 2nd. "We do not know if Britain and France will come to Poland's aid." In the meantime life was being regulated on a wartime basis. The following day Britain and France declared war on Germany, and all the dominions of the British Empire, except Ireland, followed suit. On September 5, the High Commissioner broadcast an appeal to all residents of Palestine to forget their differences in a common effort against German aggression. "We are living in something of a war atmosphere," Adele told Thomas. "Petrol and kerosene are being rationed, and people are laying in vast stores of supplies."

Despite the tense atmosphere, Henrietta continued to travel on her accustomed rounds. Benjamin wrote from Petah Tikva on November 1 to his sister Harriet Terrell:

> Last Thursday Aunt Adele came out to see us and I rode back with her to see Aunt Henrietta. We found her at Givat Ha-Shelosha, a kibbutz near Petah Tikva. She was sitting with a committee of the kibbutz discussing Youth Aliyah problems. Aunt Henrietta's department lays down conditions for the kibbutzim to follow if they want to receive children. These deal with the health, education, and employment of the child. Some of the kibbutzim do not observe their conditions strictly and then Aunt Henrietta has to get after them. It was remarkable to sit there and listen to her. She has a very firm and sure grasp of the details of the situation and was never at a

loss for an answer to the arguments of the committee. I do not know anyone who gets about so much and sees so many different settlements repeatedly. If Aunt Henrietta ever retires from organization work she ought to write a book on the Jewish settlements in Palestine.

Bertha, with constant care, was on the mend from her heart attack. She wrote to 'Dear Everybody'' at home on November 3: ''For some persons yesterday was mainly Balfour Day, but for me it meant farewell to Adele who is supposed to embark on the *Excalibur* today at Haifa. Sad as I am to have her abandon us, I think she is wholly wise to return to the States now.''

Bertha wrote to her family on December 19:

The last time Henrietta announced that a Youth Aliyah trip was in the offing, I said I was going with her, regardless of naps. Wednesday morning we set forth. Our companions were Mr. Beyth, Henrietta's *fidus Achates*, and social worker Dorothy Kahn, who was out for newspaper stories, and so made an excellent person for me to be with in order to learn a thing or two about places and people. At Haifa, lunch in a workingman's cafe, and through the Emek to Balfouria, where, after an interesting discussion of policy between Henrietta and the Youth Aliyah group, Dorothy Kahn and I left Henrietta for individual interviews.

The next day was an interesting one for which the trip was taken. A ''village'' started for religious youth of the Youth Aliyah had completed its buildings and was celebrating the occasion. The fete was an all-day affair, but we left after a dinner served to hundreds of people. At the dinner, a boy and Henrietta were the only speakers. Once dinner was over and grace said, the boys cleared the tables, put them together, and covered them with plants for a stage on which they were to give two playlets. (The girls had served the meal gracefully and deftly). The village has an enchantingly beautiful location. The houses are scattered irregularly over a hilly, stony terrain. One looks from this elevation across the neat, cultivated fields of the school, lusciously green now, to the hills of the Carmel range, wooded with oak and therefore different from the bare Judean hills hereabout.

At last Bertha was well enough to sail for home on February 12, 1940. It was a sad parting for Henrietta, but sadder news from home was even more distressing. She had received a letter telling of Adele's very serious illness: amoebic dysentery, pneumonia, and bacterial endocarditis. Adele had been rushed to Mt. Sinai Hospital in New York. "I have been living in a trance, hardly knowing what I was doing," Henrietta told Benjamin. "I work with an external brain." Adele died on March 16. The first installment of her excellent four-part article on Palestine, "The Great Will," did not appear until the October issue of *Opinion*, a Journal of Jewish Life and Letters.

Tribulation after tribulation crowded in upon Henrietta. She took a misstep and fell severely injuring one leg. This put her to bed until a badly wrenched muscle healed. It meant a temporary check on her travels, but by June 7 she could write to Benjamin:

> I got back into my full routine during the week, which means meetings galore. Most of them were connected with the emergency. There is no money, and without funds, ample funds at that, emergency plans are bound to remain on paper. All interstices of time, of course, were filled in with horror at the slaughter in Europe. In spite of all, we are actually expecting to bring groups of children here. Our refugees in Sweden, 118 in number, expect to leave Stockholm on June 15 and travel by the Russian route. They will be followed by 270 from Denmark, also by the Russian route. Nearly 300 from England may have to come via the Cape of Good Hope, Bombay, Basrah, Bagdad, and across the desert—if we can finance them! From Lithuania, Roumania, and Hungary we may be able to transport several hundred in spite of the closing of Trieste. Such are the plans. Tomorrow events may shatter them.

CHAPTER 8

THE *PATRIA* DISASTER
AND AN EIGHTIETH BIRTHDAY

On May 10, 1940, Hitler's army had invaded Holland. In June France was conquered by the Germans. "I am particularly downhearted over the news from Paris," Henrietta wrote on June 14. "What an array! Poland, Norway, Denmark, Belgium, Holland, France—all since September."

After the departure of her sisters, Henrietta had moved from the apartment to the Pension Romm, a two-story cottage of pink Jerusalem stone, No. 11 Ramban Street. She wrote on July 5:

> I feel as though I were standing in a howling desert, vast stretches of desolation on all sides. From day to day one opens the newspapers expectantly, only to be hurled into greater depths of despair. These days have convinced me that King Solomon wrote Ecclesiastes in his old age, the defeatist age. My refrain would be, instead of vanity, all is vanity—cruelty, all is cruelty.

The rescue of the children from war-torn Europe was uppermost in Henrietta's mind when she wrote on August 9:

> We are still hammering away at the problem of bringing our young candidates from Denmark, Sweden, and Lithuania. There are about 600 of them. Besides there is a group of 120 we are endeavoring to save from among the group of unfortunates who have been waiting on vessels on the Danube at the Yugoslavia border since January to be brought here as Ma'pilim—illegal aliens. We have secured all the necessary funds for the transfer of the 720, and all the visas—Russia,

49

Lithuania, Syria—except the Turkish. Now our hearts have stopped beating until the emissary sent to Turkey for the purpose, cables the Agency the result of his diplomatic intervention. Nothing daunted, however, and in expectation of our third quota of certificates for the current period, we have begun preparations for Roumanian and Hungarian groups. "Hope springs eternal!"

Upon the outbreak of war the price of food and other necessities had taken a sudden jump in Palestine. The Turko-Anglo-French treaty had greatly quieted fears, and prices dropped somewhat, but not for long. Italy's entrance into the war on the side of Germany almost entirely closed the Mediterranean to British merchant ships, while France's collapse blocked the Syrian border, producing a further strain upon Palestine's economic life.

In April 1939, the British High Commissioner was empowered to restrict immigration into Palestine on the grounds of economic and political necessity. The quota established for the period from April to September of that year provided for the entry of only 5,000 regular immigrants and 5,350 refugees. However many Jews fleeing persecution in Europe sought entry into Palestine by illegal means. Benjamin Levin had written to his sister, Harriet Terrell, on November 1, 1939:

During the months immediately preceding the war a swarm of refugees came into Palestine legally or illegally. So many came in that this year was in fact one of the banner years of Jewish immigration. Over 100 are now in Kfar Syrkin. They are camped in tents on a vacant lot. Finding work for them is one of the great problems of this locality. We have had several of them help us in work. They come from all countries in Eastern and Central Europe. One girl who helped Sarah with housework for a short time explained to us why most of them had practically nothing at all. The boat landed them on some desolate part of the coast where there was no dock of any sort. They had to walk a long way through water to get to land, and then they had to throw away most of what little they had brought with them.

Despite the restrictions on entry certificates and the problems of transportation during wartime, Henrietta labored on for the Youth Aliyah. She wrote on August 23, 1940:

My spirit is sore, as must be the spirit of every thinking and feeling human being in this troubled world. One plucks up courage for a moment on reading a Churchill speech. It's only a passing emotion at best. We haven't yet succeeded in bringing to Palestine a single child on the certificates of the present half-year. One obstacle after the other has interposed itself. At present it is Turkey's refusal to grant visas after we secured, with infinite trouble, visas from Russia, Lithuania, and Syria. We believe it is the only obstacle left.

During the first week of October Henrietta spent two very hot days near Tel Aviv, one forenoon in Naan, a kibbutz near Rehovot, and an afternoon in Zichron Meir. She wrote on October 9:

The influence of the times upon our youth groups is marked. There is a suppressed excitement among them, with frequent rebellious outbursts. Sometimes the feelings are assuaged by the mobilization of the leaders. Oftener the group indulges in complaints and nurses imaginary and actual grievances. I have had to quell incipient rebellions in several places—a difficult job with heat inside and outside. The last Khamsin days during the holidays were unbearable.

On November 4, 1940, Franklin D. Roosevelt was re-elected as president of the United States. Four days later Henrietta noted that in Jerusalem people were "jubilant."

Meanwhile the volume of illegal immigration into Palestine had become so large that drastic steps were taken to curtail it. The British continued to reduce immigration quotas and threatened to deport any persons attempting to enter Palestine without proper certification. In England Colonel Josiah Wedgwood, an eminent Laborite member of Parliament, protested vigorously against his Government's policy of immigration quotas for Palestine. He pointed out that the illegal Jewish refugees were anxious and able to aid Great Britain, in the army, workshops and fields of Palestine. Five thousand Jews enlisted in the British forces.

Early in November 1940, two steamers, *Milos* and *Pacific*, arrived in Haifa carrying 1,771 illegal refugees from Central Europe. On November 20 it was announced that these people would be deported to some British colony and interned there for the duration of the war. At war's end they would not be allowed to remain in the colony, nor could they go to Palestine. The 1,771 passengers were transferred on board the 12,000-ton French liner, *Patria*, which the British had chartered to deport the group to the island of Mauritius. The *Patria* lay in Haifa harbor awaiting a favorable opportunity to depart. On the morning of November 25 the passengers of the *Atlantic,* another ship carrying 1,800 illegal immigrants, were being transferred to the *Patria* when a tragedy occurred. Some 130 of the *Atlantic's* passengers were already aboard the *Patria* when the latter vessel blew up and sank within fifteen minutes in Haifa Bay. Around 260 persons lost their lives; 209 bodies were eventually recovered. The disaster was caused by the ignition of explosives brought aboard in an attempt to sabotage the engines and thus prevent the refugee's deportation. The survivors of the *Patria* were permitted by the British to remain in Palestine as ''an exceptional act of mercy,'' and were interned for some time at a detention camp at Athlit. The remaining passengers of the *Atlantic,* about 1,600 refugees mostly from Austria, Czechoslovakia and Poland, were deported to Mauritius. The British deducted the number of *Patria* refugees allowed to remain in the country from the next legal immigration quota.*

The dead from the *Patria* were buried with solemn rites in Haifa. All Jewish shops, factories and schools were shut during the funeral. Henrietta wrote on November 28, three days after the tragedy:

> The week has been filled with the Haifa catastrophe. First, all thoughts were centered on provisions for the comfort of the deportees and then on clothing the naked. The collection of clothing, underwear and shoes in Jerusalem was a notable feat. It was the first task applied to our *She'at herum* organization devised for war emergency purposes. It stood the test admirably. Within a few hours Jerusalem could send over 10,000 pieces of clothing and shoes to Haifa—4,000 by Hadassah, the rest by the volunteer collectors in the 14 districts into which the Sherut-ha-Am of the Social Service Department of the city (Kehillah) had divided Jerusalem. But the last message is that more is needed. Of our Youth Aliyah candidates—there were 77 on board—one lost his life and, it appears, four girls are missing. The report is that the wrecked boat still holds a number of victims.

That same week, however, brought the good news that one of the Youth Aliyah groups from Scandinavia was about to embark. ''We may expect them here by the end of December,'' Henrietta wrote. ''About 1200 more are waiting in various European countries with

---

*Encyclopedia Judaica (Jerusalem: Keter Publishing House 1971), Vol.   13, p. 181

their certificates in hand.'' She wrote again on December 6:

> This week, too, has been consumed by the *Patria* incident. Not that
> anything was achieved. But one was trying to achieve. Now we are
> living in hopes that at least the young people and the children will
> be permitted to leave the camps at Athlit and wherever they may be,
> and be taken care of by us. Places are ready for them.

Yet the *Patria* tragedy did not change the British Government's policy.
On December 8, 1,584 recently arrived illegal immigrants were
deported.

On December 13, Henrietta returned from a three-day trip to the
Emek Ha-Yarden settlements. She and her faithful assistant, Hans
Beyth, had made Tiberias their headquarters, sallying forth from there
each day. They visited Ashdot Ya'acov, a kibbutz where Henrietta was
photographed walking with and instructing an attractive young
women, Yael Goldfarb, a Youth Aliyah graduate who was taking a
third year of training at Ashdot Ya'acov. Other settlements were
visited, and Henrietta considered the trip one of her most successful
and enjoyable ones because the Ha-Yarden settlements were in so
flourishing a state. All of them had been embellished and incredibly
improved in the course of the year since she was last there. Their
increased prosperity seemed due in part to the industrial enterprises
which had been added to their agricultural undertakings. ''Within the
next ten days we expect the arrival of Youth Aliyah candidates from
Denmark and a small group of refugees from Constantinople.''
Henrietta wrote on December 14. ''We also have hopes of securing the
release of over seventy from the Athlit camps.''

Henrietta dreaded the approach of her eightieth birthday, and
wondered whether she would survive the impending celebrations
with their eulogies. She did not consider herself a heroine, yet adula-
tion came her way. *The New York Times Magazine* for December 15, 1940,
paid her a tribute in an article titled ''Grand Old Lady of Palestine.''
''For what she has contributed to mankind her name is blessed in
various tongues the world around,'' wrote Kathleen McLaughlin.
''Since the days of her youth Miss Szold has launched social welfare
activities in such profusion that her name ranks with that of Jane
Addams of Hull House...or Lilliam Wald of Henry Street.''

According to the *Baltimore Sun* for February 14, 1945, Henrietta's
eightieth birthday was honored in five hundred American cities and in
various other countries by local Jewish groups. And the Women's

Centennial Congress cited her as one of the one hundred outstanding women of the past century.

Meanwhile at the children's village of Ben Shemen on the road to Lod, young men and women who had graduated from the Youth Aliyah, as well as boys and girls still in training, gathered to honor Henrietta on her landmark birthday. They represented the nearly 8,000 youngsters whom the Youth Aliyah had rescued from Europe's holocaust.

One young Austrian girl told Geveret Szold: "We will follow the road we have taken, forward and upward. And you will be on that road." Henrietta wrote to her nephew Benjamin on January 23, 1941:

> You ask about the Ben Shemen celebration and add an inquiry about the Hadassah celebration. I have been saying that they were the high points. I think the reason is that in both the celebration was carried by the young. At the Hadassah celebration there was first a dinner with the doctors and graduate nurses, at which many of the earliest co-workers of mine, who have long ago left the Hadassah work, had a reunion, and we all indulged in reminiscences. Afterwards, at the Nurses' Training School, there were tableaux depicting the development of Hadassah from the inception of the plan thirty-one years ago when my mother and I were in Palestine on a visit. One of the nurses gave a running commentary—very clever. Then there was a jollification.
>
> There were two more "features" that are to be cherished. The Vaad Leumi arranged a school children's broadcast hour which I opened with a brief reflection. It was well done—the children's part—depicting various episodes in my life. To the older pupils a pamphlet was given throughout the country giving my biography. On my recent trip to Mishmar Ha-Emek, where I met the Danish group who have at last reached Palestine, I was everywhere greeted by the children, the little ones belonging to the settlements, with the outcry that they had heard me on the radio.

Henrietta had broadcast the following message to the children:

> When I was your age, there was no telephone, no motorcar, no airplane, and even no radio. Now, when I have grown old, I am privileged, due to that wonderful invention, radio, to make my voice heard by the thousands of boys and girls in all corners of Palestine. You can see with your own eyes how many and won-

rous are the changes which have come to this world in the 80 years of my life. But one thing has not changed, nor has time affected. Generous men and women do good deeds. Today, like yesterday, educated men and women think great thoughts. Today, like yesterday, active men and women work and create...

CHAPTER 9

"HENRIETTA SZOLD: LIFE AND LETTERS"

For Henrietta one high point of her eightieth birthday was the transfer to the Hebrew University Library of the manuscripts of her beloved father's scholarly *Commentary on the Book of Job*. She described the event for Benjamin, her father's namesake, on January 23, 1941:

> From a certain point of view the crowning celebration was the one at the University last Friday morning. Dr. Magnes had invited me to be there at eleven o'clock with the case of mss. He sent a taxi for me. To my surprise I was ushered into a room in the Library in which were assembled all the professors and instructors in the Department of Jewish Studies.

Among the scholars who greeted her was Martin Buber, professor of social philosophy, whose works emphasized the cultural significance of Judaism. There was also Professor Gotthold Weil, a Berlin-born Orientalist, who held the chair of Turkish studies. Another scholar present was Leon Roth, a PhD. from Oxford, who was Rector at the University and professor of philosophy. Henrietta felt honored by the assemblage of distinguished men of letters. Dr. Magnes spoke of the manuscripts and of her father, Dr. Benjamin Szold. Then Henrietta was asked to tell something of the circumstances under which Dr. Szold had written the *Commentary*. Altogether it was a most impressive meeting. Henrietta added: "Dr. Magnes also announced that there were already candidates for the prize he had offered—a circumstance due primarily one must admit to the poverty of the students—rather than to their interest in Job or Hebrew poetry."

The one fly in the ointment of Henrietta's pleasure at the birthday celebration which refused to end was that she had been unable to thank the 900 people who had greeted her with flowers and gifts. And she had been flooded with letters from strangers congratulating her but using their felicitations to petition for work, money and positions. But by February 21 she could write: "This week has brought us good news." One cable, from Roumania, announced the coming of 235 Youth Aliyah candidates, while a second one from Stockholm said that Turkey had granted visas to 50 more. "During the week, too, we celebrated the seventh anniversary of the arrival of our first group."

On June 22, 1941, Hitler invaded the Soviet Union. Meanwhile Henrietta and her colleagues continued their struggle to save Europe's hounded young. The children's emotional, as well as physical, needs demanded attention. On one trip Henrietta and Hans Beyth had picked up a runaway who had asked for a lift in their auto. The lad, aged twelve and a half, had on a large backpack filled with all his possessions. By day's end they had returned him safely to his own school. Henrietta wrote on July 18:

> This week was absorbed, so far as my thoughts and my planning are concerned, by a runaway Youth Aliyah boy. We had been treating him psychiatrically for over a year and a half, and we flattered ourselves with success. Recruiting fever counteracted all we had done. In a few minutes he ought to be here, for me to begin all over again. Will he come? The world unrest has not left youth unaffected!

Henrietta had other concerns, among them the still interned *Patria* survivors. She wrote on July 25:

> Yesterday I paid a visit to the camp at Athlit. In recent weeks we were permitted to take out 115 children and young people and care for them through the Youth Aliyah. Now a number of additional children have been transferred from the second camp at Mazon, near Acco, to Athlit, and we are hoping something may be done to release them to us, too. Among the 96 now there, about 47 are of the age the Youth Aliyah can deal with. The rest are too young.
>
> I was permitted contact with the adults, too. Black despair and hopelessness! They have been deprived of liberty these eight months. While the conditions in the camp are not too bad, the monotony of their days and its lack of purpose and aim bring them to the very edge of insanity. *Hinaus, hinaus!* they all cry, even the

little boys and girls of six and seven, of course in imitation of their elders. What is heartrending is the cry of the members of the disrupted families: the mother has been released, the children remain behind; the father is at the other camp, the mother and children at Athlit; the father has been in the country several years, the wife and children remain in detention. They expect me to speak to the High Commissioner! Utterly useless, I am convinced.

Hadassah, then 94,000 strong, had given Henrietta $25,000 as a birthday gift to use as she saw fit. She decided that it should fund the organization of three groups of urban children to be modeled on the Youth Aliyah groups. She wrote on August 15:

I returned late last evening from a two days' trip to Haifa and the Emek region. My business was to inspect the two camps we have organized for the purpose of choosing sixty city children to whom we are to give an opportunity for agricultural education or adjustment parallel to the Youth Aliyah system. There will be three groups, twenty boys and girls in each. In large part they consist of children of the Eastern communities. I believe we have made a successful beginning of what promises to be a valuable contribution to educational development. We found the children at both places happy, primarily I think, because without let or hindrance they were eating their fill of good food.

A day earlier, on August 14, Prime Minister Winston Churchill of Great Britain and President Franklin D. Roosevelt of the United States announced a joint program of peace aims. The statement, an unofficial document, was drawn up at sea off the coast of Newfoundland. Henrietta wrote on the 25th: "After Churchill's Atlantic Charter address, and the news that the British and Russians are in Iran, I should be satisfied, if not pleased with the present."

The death of her good friend, Louis D. Brandeis, a justice of the United States Supreme Court and a leading Zionist, was a sad occasion for Henrietta. She wrote on October 11: I was kept particularly busy the past week by newspapers and broadcasts in connection with the passing of Mr. Brandeis. During the coming week, too, I shall have to prepare two tributes, one for the meeting of the Zionist Actions Committee, the second for a memorial meeting to be arranged by Ein Ha-Shofet." Ein Ha-Shofet, the kibbutz named for Mr. Brandeis, means "The Judge's Spring," and is located in the Manasseh Hills west of Megiddo.

The day before the death of Justice Brandeis, Henrietta had attended the funeral of Menachem Ussishkin, a member of the Zionist Executive. Thousands of persons had followed his bier. Henrietta described the occasion:

> Mr. Ussishkin's funeral was an impressive demonstration. It is difficult for me to adjust myself to a Jerusalem without Mr. Ussishkin. He was a Rock of Gibraltar. People say there is no one to fill his place. Perhaps there is no replica of him but, in spite of the torn world we live in, I hold to what we read today in Kohelet— generations come, and generations go, but the world stands firm. I believe, too, that Mr. Brandeis, of the two, was still a living, stimulating influence, while Mr. Ussishkin seems to me to have made his impress years ago and has not added to it since many a day.

Soon another death occurred which shocked Henrietta. Professor David Yellin, an educator whom she had known for thirty-two years, died suddenly.

"I suppose old age is bound to have the effect of slowing down the processes of living and working, and doubtless it takes me longer than it used to to do the day's work," she wrote on December 15. "I am equally sure, however, that my day's stint goes on growing in content and extent—I simply cannot keep pace with what is expected of me." Yet Henrietta was remarkably spry and fit for her years. At the age of eighty-one she was photographed dancing the Horah, a popular folk dance, with a group of Youth Aliyah youngsters.

A bout of influenza coupled with bronchitis felled her for a time, but by January 5, 1942, Dr. Magnes could cable New York Hadassah that her condition was satisfactory. Hadassah relayed the welcome news to Bertha Levin at Baltimore. By January 20 Henrietta herself was well enough to write to Benjamin:

> I believe I may say that I have recovered in all but strength. I think if the weather became milder, less windy, that I could regularly perambulate on the street for a half hour daily, I might gain more quickly. The day nurse left me only two days ago. Now I need the sun without wind. I saw nothing of the snow which everybody went crazy about. I was tucked away under the bed covers the whole time.
>
> I am sending you, under separate cover, three documents which

will explain my plan, "Le-Maan Ha-Yeled Ve-Ha-Noar," on which I worked for a number of years. There is a Trust Deed, the Rules of Association, and my Introduction which I delivered in transmitting the plan to the Vaad Leumi. The delivery was made on my birthday when, it turned out, I was already sick with a rather high fever.

Henrietta's plan for the Vaad Leumi's Fund for Child and Youth Care dealt with the needs of the youth of the entire community, embracing education, health and social service. It included school hygiene, summer camps, playgrounds, kindergartens, vocational education, correctional institutions, and other concerns.

Henrietta was encouraged when the Government granted Youth Aliyah 250 certificates out of the 3000 allotted to that period. In addition the authorities for the first time gave permission for boys and girls up to sixteen years of age minus one day to be brought out from enemy-occupied territory—from Roumania and Hungary. And there was some hope that they might be able to take the children off the *Struma,* a ship loaded with illegal immigrants from Roumania. The ship had been warned not to approach the shore of Palestine and was turned back from Constantinople. It sank in the Black Sea, taking with it some 800 refugees. Henrietta wrote on February 28:

> I had a hard day yesterday. We all had a hard day on account of the *Struma* disaster. We of the Youth Aliyah had had high hopes of saving the children from suffering on that miserable ship. We could not save them from a horrible end. I suffered doubly and trebly because in fulfilment of a promise long ago given I visited the passengers of the *Dorian* detained at Athlit. They were fasting to express their sympathy with the fate of fellow-sufferers. I came back physically exhausted. Then, too, the children were my chief concern. There is not much hope that even they will be liberated. Think of it! There are 19 little babies there born as it were in captivity!

The coming of Passover, *Z'man herutenu,* the season of our liberation, brought further problems for Henrietta. She wrote on April 3:

> I should have been particularly attuned to the festival of the Redemption, because I had a part in the release of thirty children from the Clearance Camp in Athlit, passengers of the S.S. *Darien,* on the way to Palestine these sixteen months: five of them on the high seas in a crazy craft and eleven months in the Camp. They were

released Tuesday forenoon by the High Commissioner who waived certain formalities in order that we might get them to their new homes for the Seder. In eighteen homes Mr. Beyth achieved the miracle. During the short time at our disposal he took two trips from Jerusalem to Athlit and back, and got the whole of them to five institutions in good time, he returning to his own Seder rather late. A second exodus from slavery to freedom! I was excited and exhausted.

"My duties overflow the limits of the hours of work, and my endurance is not what it was," Henrietta admitted on April 17. "I have long known that I should jump from the bandwagon—it moves too fast—but I can't find the proper moment for jumping down without, as it were, breaking my leg or breaking the backbone of whatever job I may be abandoning."

Two days later *The New York Times Book Review* printed a critique of *Henrietta Szold: Life and Letters,* published by the Viking Press under the auspices of Hadassah. The review's headline read: "Marvin Lowenthal's Life of the Dauntless Woman Whose Name is Linked with Palestine." Earlier, on April 5, the *New York Herald Tribune Books* section termed the book "a discriminating biography of a memorable woman."

At Baltimore, Henrietta's hometown, the Enoch Pratt Free Library displayed Lowenthal's book in one of its large windows facing on Cathedral Street. Miss Kate Coplan, the library's talented publicity expert, had arranged copies of the book intermixed with Szold memorabilia. There was a charming framed oval pastel portrait of Henrietta as a child of six or seven, wearing a dainty pink dress. There were photos of her parents and of the houses lived in by the family. In the center was a long chain of diverse fancy buttons strung on a stout cord. A photograph of the display was sent to Henrietta who wrote on May 15:

That Enoch Pratt Library window exhibit is enjoyable even to me with all my objection to publicity, from which I have suffered all the days of my life—almost. I think exhibiting that string of buttons is a stroke of genius. It is essentially mid-Victorian. The string is over five yards long and represents button collections made by several members of the family, beginning with me, going on to my sister Rachel, and from her to my sister Sadie. They are strung on their shanks, and there was a "touch button." Whoever, in handling the string, happened to touch the fatal button, had to contribute a button to the string, different in design from any on the string. I still remember my "touch button." It was milky white china, with a swallow designed on it.

Nevertheless I look forward to the book itself with trepidation, in spite of the series of letters I have had from friends praising the book extravagantly. I can understand Harry Friedenwald's judgment— his admiration of Marvin Lowenthal's literary craftsmanship. The book is to be brought to me by a member of the U.S. forces soon to come to Palestine.

The book finally arrived, and Henrietta wrote to the author, Marvin Lowenthal, from the Pension Romm on June 22:

This afternoon Dr. Magnes brought me "the book" about which my sister had been writing to me and a score of friends, all in the same major key of admiration of what you had woven out of an endless skein of letters of mine. . . . the volume lies before me on my desk, with its two gracious inscriptions, the one from you, and the other from my Hadassah associates, in the name of one hundred thousand women.

After some preliminary apprehension, Henrietta enjoyed reading Lowenthal's book although she did not regard herself as a fit subject for biography. A year earlier, the Jewish Publication Society had brought out *I Have Considered the Days*, the autobiographical memoir of Dr. Cyrus Adler, president of Dropsie College and the Jewish Theological Seminary in New York. Dr. Adler, three years younger than Henrietta, had died in 1940. She wrote of the two books:

In my opinion Cyrus Adler's reminiscences are as imperfect as my *Life and Letters*. However, it at least touches upon the core of one aspect of the life which he and I experienced. We were both contemporaneous with the consolidation of Jewish life in the United States—with its advance from infancy, as it were, to the age of self-consciousness. In part that makes itself felt in his badly-ordered, rather drily arranged incidents and interests. But it does not appear as a movement. And he personally played no small role in this development.

Henrietta had more pressing things on her mind when she wrote on August 28:

> My work had been devoted to one thing—thinking out how we are going to meet the problem presented to us by a cable from Teheran which announces that five hundred chiefly parentless children have come across the Russo-Persian border, sick, starved, degenerate after endless wanderings. They are between the ages of five and ten. The first demand is certificates, the second, oodles of money. I am not altogether certain that the Youth Aliyah is the agency to deal with the present situation. And if it is, am I the person to preside over such an enlarged agency—enlarged not by reason of increased numbers, but by reason of increased and deepened scope.

A week later she had spoken to a group of Egyptian evacuees at the first of a series of talks to be given them under the auspices of the Jewish Agency, the Vaad Leumi, and the WIZO. "I suppose it is a praise-worthy attempt to interest the Egyptian visitors in Palestinian problems," she commented. "The Jews in Egypt, right next door to us, have never entered wholeheartedly into our troubles and our joys."

The day after Pearl Harbor the United States had entered the war on December 8, 1941. Henrietta had heard that already American soldiers in numbers were in Tel Aviv. The expanded war made her chance of getting home to America increasingly dim.

CHAPTER 10

THE TEHERAN CHILDREN ARRIVE

In the autumn of 1942 Henrietta had a distinguished visitor, Wendell
L. Willkie, the defeated Republican candidate for president of the
United States. Mr. Willkie had switched from the Democratic Party
because of his antagonism to the New Deal. Nominated by the
Republicans to challenge Roosevelt, Willkie had endorsed the latter's
foreign policy during the campaign of 1940 while attacking his
domestic policy. Now, as President Roosevelt's personal representative, he was on a tour to England, Egypt, the Near East, Russia and
China to sound out the leaders on a possible peace for the world. On his
"One World" tour Willkie spend one full day in Palestine, and in spite
of his limited time, called on Henrietta. She wrote on September 20:

> Mr. Willkie's visit to me was most interesting. The distinction was
> accorded to me, I think, because Dr. Magnes was not in town. I have
> reason to believe that Mr. Lowell Pinkerton, the American Consul,
> routed him to me. Dr. Magnes, as I know because he had consulted
> me on it, had written a letter to Mr. Willkie on the subject of the
> Polish refugees in Russia, and how it might be arranged to get at the
> true facts—there are rumors without cease. In Dr. Magnes's absence
> over the holiday, the Consul was to get the letter to Mr. Willkie who
> had come this way primarily to visit Russia.
>
> At noon on Erev Rosh Ha-Shanah, I was called up at the office by
> Mr. Scott, who was the Acting Chief Secretary, and told that Mr.
> Willkie desired to speak to me, would I come for tea to the High
> Commissioner's—not the usual preparations for one of the High
> Holidays. However, I believe an invitation from the High Commis-
> sioner is tantamount to a command. Hence I accepted. About an
> hour later, Mr. Scott called again to tell me that Mr. Willkie preferred

to meet me at my own home. Auch Recht! He came at four o'clock, accompanied by three men, one of them a photographer, one in uniform (but I can't tell you of what country or what service), and a third, just a plain man. They were introduced to me by name, but the names meant nothing to me, and, as usual, they were glossed over, vulgo, mumbled, and if I heard them, I promptly forgot them.

Mr. Willkie at once launched into his subject. He briefly gave me the gist of conversations he had with the High Commissioner, the high point of which was that the two peoples in Palestine, the Jews and the Arabs, were politically immature, hence democratic, liberal institutions cannot yet be granted them. This is not to be repeated! Mr. Willkie then said that he was of the opinion that America must be a prime factor in settling the world order in the post-war period, that the Jewish problem was an outstanding question, and its Palestine solution an important element, and hence the Arab-Jewish relation interested him. What was the solution? He stuck to this subject for the whole time he was with me, all of three quarters of an hour. He questioned me closely about the Arabs and the Government. I got the impression that he has not informed himself profoundly on any aspect of the Jewish problem, but that he has the vigorous, open mind which would enable him to immerse himself in it to our advantage, or, at least, on the side of justice. The atmosphere in my room was breezily American.

In justice to Dr. Magnes, and because I am deeply interested in the Russian situation as it affects our refugees I did my best to divert him to this problem. He would not be diverted. I kept it a dark secret from him that Dr. Magnes and I and all who are interested in the Ichud are being hunted down. Have you seen that some of our patriots want to read me out of the Zionist Organization?

The Ichud, an organization whose aims Henrietta and Dr. Magnes favored, had the twofold program of seeking rapprochement between Jews and Arabs, and of advocating the idea of binationalism. Despite the opinion of some of the Jewish "patriots" that followers of Ichud were naive, Wendell Willkie's appraisal of Henrietta was that she had more wisdom about the problems of Palestine and elsewhere than all the civil servants and politicians.

Henrietta's thoughts were absorbed by the task ahead of bringing to Palestine over 900 Polish refugee children waiting at Pahlevi, the Persian port on the Caspian Sea. These children, after three years of wandering following the Nazi invasion of Poland, had finally arrived at a refugee camp near Teheran. By early September 1942, Henrietta had not yet succeeded in obtaining the necessary certificates but she refused to be anything but hopeful. She and her colleagues had received word in writing that the Polish authorities would grant them three pounds per month per child for the duration of the war. And Hadassah's reply to Henrietta's appeal held out a handsome promise of hope. She wrote on October 16:

> My sole interest at the moment is the children in Teheran. The more I enter into the details of the task, the better I realize the difficulties we are facing. This week the Mitzvah chasers opened new problem vistas before me. The Agudat Israel sets up the claim that these children from Poland doubtless belong to it. But the Mizrachi Organization claims no less. Then come the parties and the institutions, and the individuals with theories and projects. How are we going to do justice to them all? How are we going to avoid doing injustice to the children?

In late November Henrietta spent two days away from Jerusalem arranging for temporary reception places for the Teheran children. About 350 of these had been secured. She described the situation on the 21st:

> We had to seek places which offered kitchen and dining room accommodations ready-made. Every plate and glass costs fortunes these days. The places secured are not sufficient for the 933 children waiting at Teheran. We are hoping that they will come, not all at once, but in age groups, so as to give us a chance to dispose of a number of them before their successors appear. So far as certificates are concerned, we could bring out 1000 children from France, and hundreds from Holland and Bulgaria, whence cries of distress reach us. But there is Hitler, and there are blocked routes, and there is no money! Meanwhile the descriptions that come through are inconceivable.

Henrietta wrote again on December 11:

> During the past week luck would have it that I was brought in contact with one of the "exchanges" from Poland, a mother of three children, who succeeded in bringing with her only one of them; the other two had disappeared according to the well-known formula worked out by the Gestapo. From her I heard details so gruesome

that I cannot recover by balance. Meanwhile the children waiting at Teheran do not receive a transit visa from the Iraqian Government. So they suffer from the cruel (so I am told) Persian winter. The children at Teheran are the only subject I can think about.

A pleasant interlude interrupted Henrietta's worries when on December 21, her eighty-second birthday, the Henrietta Szold Forest was planted at Maaleh Hahamisha, a kibbutz near the Jerusalem-Tel Aviv highway. Henrietta, surrounded by a crowd of friends and well-wishers, planted the first and eighty-third tree. Then she sat in a chair provided for her on the rough ground while messages of congratulation were read.

In addition to the Henrietta Szold Forest, Henrietta had a kibbutz named after her. Kfar Szold, formerly located in the south, had obtained permanent land in the far north near Dan, in the Hula Valley on the Syrian border.

The New Year brought fresh worries for Henrietta who wrote on January 31, 1943:

> I must admit that the Teheran children are overwhelming me—not they, really, but the people who are desperately interested in their welfare—the Poles resident in Palestine, who are of the opinion that, though possibly I may know how to deal with German youth and children, or those from Austria, Czechoslovakia, Bulgaria, Roumania, Italy, Yugoslavia, Latvia, and the two or three hundred Poles whom I brought in clandestinely, I cannot be trusted to take care of the Polish refugee children. And the Agudat Israel and the Mizrachi have constituted themselves the keepers of their souls. Even without the endless discussions I am compelled to carry on with these doubters of my competence.

Meanwhile many persons became involved in diplomatic maneuvers to free the Teheran children. The wife of U.S. Secretary of the Treasury Henry Morgenthau played a part, as did Mrs. Eleanor Roosevelt. Sumner Welles and others of the U.S. State Department, the American Red Cross, the U.S. Army, the Iraqui at Washington, and Lord Halifax, the British Ambassador to Washington, were also caught up in the undertaking. At last a ship took the children from Persia to Karachi and them to Port Suez where they arrived on February 17. Henrietta had sent Hans Beyth to meet them, and the next day, when they are taken to the Athlit Clearance Camp, she was ther to greet them. She wrote on February 28:

> The Teheran children! I was in Haifa-Athlit for nine days full to
> repletion. If my Athlit days were full, the dictionary offers no word
> conveying adequately what my days are now. Chiefly I tell people,
> curiosity-mongers, that they can't visit the children and interview
> them. The whole country seems to have gone plumb crazy. The
> children's arival was an historic event, I admit. I should like to have
> the leisure to write up a full description of all the attendant cir-
> cumstances. It would, indeed, make a document for the histories of
> the future.

In their years of hopeless wandering as they were hounded from place
to place, the children had slept in woods, had bordered on starvation,
and were exposed to disease. Clothed in near-rags, these wild,
frightened young ones needed a great deal of attention, both physical
and psychological. "The past week I have continued the individual
examinations," Henrietta explained on April 10. "If my health were
up to the mark, I should doubtless find the conversations illuminating.
At all events, they reveal a state of degeneration among our tortured
people that cannot but arouse anxiety."
  Things looked a bit brighter when she wrote again on June 18:

> I spent the week rushing hither and thither, and succeeded prac-
> tically in completing the survey of the Teheran children in their per-
> manent placements. On the whole I am pleased with what I have
> seen of them. They are apparently making good progress toward
> normality. They study with vim. Most of them have already
> acquired enough Hebrew to carry on a conversation. They are no
> less ready to do the work assigned to them. What pleases me most
> is that they are beginning to frolic, to be children. They will snatch
> back a little of the heritage of youth that the Hitler war robbed them
> of.

WELL-DESERVED RECOGNITION

The war ground on. German submarines sank Allied ships at an unprecedented rate, and a gigantic offensive against Stalingrad had been launched. The Allies' first decisive blow against the Axis came when the British under General Montgomery routed Rommel at Alamein in North Africa. Then on November 8, 1942, the Americans invaded Algeria. In this action the Americans and British were joined by French forces under General de Gaulle.

In late January 1943, Henrietta sent her nephew Benjamin a clipping from the *Palestine Post* which announced that American citizens living in Palestine could volunteer for service in the U.S. Army. An enlistment office was opened in Tel Aviv, and Benjamin offered his services. His enlistment was accepted and he arranged to take his oath on April 27. He wrote to his brother Jastrow on May 4:

> My whole life has changed suddenly and radically. At present my artillery consists of a battery of typewriter keys and the hand grenades I sling around are bulky files. I have the distinction of being a private in a camp where nearly everybody is an officer or at least an NCO. Instead of worrying over how to throw bombs at Germans my biggest worry is how to know when to salute an officer.
>
> I don't know whether I am in Palestine or America. I can say "Presto, Vanish America!" and I am among Valencia oranges, Histadrut members, Hebrew, German and Yiddish conversation; and then I can say "Abracadabra" and I am among Old Golds, Camels, fig newtons, gingersnaps, *The New Yorker*, and middle

Western twang. Right now I am in Pittsburgh and not Nahalal.

Henrietta was still making her rounds, traveling hither and yon with her assistant, Hans Beyth. One day had been spent at Meir Shefeyah, a children's village on Mount Carmel, where they visited the Iraqi-Syrian group of Youth Aliyah and a new Aden Yemenite group. There they had a guest, a distinguished Swiss journalist, who was gathering material for a series of articles on Palestine. He was deeply impressed by what he had seen.

Henrietta wrote July 16:

> I am buried under details crowding in upon my attention. It's not only Youth Aliyah that makes constant demands upon my time and strength. I wonder whether there is a single person in Palestine who suffers, or whose children suffer, or who is out of work who doesn't turn to me. I can help very, very few, and the fact that my answers perforce are negative in the large majority of cases is a drain upon my mental and emotional strength.
>
> I was away from Jerusalem Wednesday and Thursday, returning last evening. My trip this time was devoted to quelling discontent in a moshav, in a Palestinian group. Initially the boys and girls resist going into a moshav. It is the kibbutz that wears the halo of romance. There is besides the difficulty of adjustment to an individual family. Many of the families are not prepared intellectually for the duty of training the adolescent youths. In Beit Shearim the only solution was to take the youths out of the moshav and assign them to various kibbutzim. The rest of my trip was devoted to visits to families and individuals, relatives of Teheran children who have accepted them as members of their families. It was interesting.

Meanwhile the war raged on. Early in May Africa had been cleared of Axis forces, and July and August saw the Allied conquest of Sicily. Refugee children still poured into Palestine.

Henrietta wrote on September 4:

> I was in Haifa from Monday until Thursday evening attending to the 108 Polish children who arrived from Teheran yesterday a week ago. They were taken to Athlit, stayed there only on Saturday, and then were transferred to Ahava, all but 23 for whom there was no room there.
>
> As quickly as could be, they were settled, and those who could not

Window display at the Enoch Pratt Free Library, Baltimore, April 1942, of Marvin Lowenthal's book, *Henrietta Szold: Life and Letters,* commissioned by Hadassah. Note the button chain in center of lower photo. Henrietta's "touch button" was of "milky white china with a swallow designed on it."

Planting of Henrietta Szold Forest at Maaleh Hachamishah on the occasion of her 82nd birthday, December 21, 1942. Miss Szold chats with friends after planting the first and eighty-third tree.

Henrietta Szold attending tea for American Red Cross workers and U.S. military personnel at the Jerusalem home of Mr. Julius Simon. Mr. Frank Tweedy of the Red Cross holds Miss Szold's arm, 1943.

be assigned at once to their permanent places were transferred to Ahava as soon as places could be cleaned. In spite of our mighty efforts and the removal of Ahava from the city, the propagandists found their way to the children and did as much mischief as they could in spite of our vigilance. The children themselves also made even greater demands than the previous group, and were rebellious because they were not getting the same public reception as their predecessors. We succeeded however in interviewing 90; only 18 are left to be interviewed. But we could settle only 43 due to the lack of religious places, especially for the little children of whom there is a large number.

Henrietta had two American visitors who wanted to see her—why she did not know. But she found it an enjoyable incident. One visitor was named Jack Benny, a movie actor. The other was Larry Adler, a virtuoso on the harmonica from Baltimore. "I had never heard of them," Henrietta explained. "And today Erica Mann, a war correspondent and daughter of Thomas Mann, came in. A breath from another world." Another visitor was young Edward Cone of Baltimore. "The Cone family was very close to me," Henrietta wrote. "They lived on Lombard Street opposite to us, and one of the daughters was my schoolmate. I fancy the young man must be the son or descendant of Caesar Cone; he and his older brother went to North Carolina and established large industries there." Henrietta's nephew Benjamin had met young Edward Cone at the U.S. Army camp.

"Our work at the office has grown gigantically; we have 2500 children and youths in training," Henrietta wrote on September 17. "They are difficult material—the Teheran children—as well as the Turkish immigration which we have been receiving lately."

In mid-September Henrietta and Hans Beyth were accompanied on their trip by Norman Bentwich who was writing a book on the Youth Aliyah and was particularly desirous of seeing the way the graduates of the movement had settled themselves. Bentwich, a writer and member of a prominent Anglo-Jewish family, had known Henrietta for a long time. During the years that she was a secretary-editor of the Jewish Publication Society he had found her to be the most "accurate" editor he had ever known. His book on the youth Aliyah was to be published by Victor Gollancz. The trio visited some seven or eight settlements and Bentwich saw all stages of the Youth Aliyah, from training to full independence. "And he was very enthusiastic," Henrietta recorded on September 24.

"So was I. I also welcomed the opportunity of seeing the settled groups whom we rarely can visit." Bentwich was still traveling with Henrietta in October when she wrote on the 13th: "Youth Aliyah has become very exacting. It bristles with demands and problems, and those ideal days in which I was mistress of the situation, without interference from the public and its leaders, are in the past."

Norman Bentwich, in his autobiographical *My Seventy-Seven Years** recalled his trips with Henrietta, then in her eighty-third year:

> A day with Miss Szold was an experience of physical and intellectual vitality. We would start early from Jerusalem, drive a hundred miles, stopping on the way at a village center to talk with a director here or a group of instructors there. At our destination we would have a meeting with a group of youths and discuss their problems. She would talk with them individually, and to the children together, in an exact Hebrew. Then on to another village; during the drive she would seem to be asleep and lost to the world. But when we arrived, she would wake and switch on the self-dynamo, and again settle all the problems. So to a third village, which we would reach after sunset, stumbling through the courtyard in the blackout. Again she would meet the whole community, adults and youths, in the dining room; again speeches, and a conference, or, if it were the end of a year's apprenticeship, an entertainment. To round off the day we would drive to Haifa or Tel Aviv, and arrive near midnight, with orders to be ready on the morrow at 7 A.M.

On October 16 Henrietta attended a tea at the Jerusalem home of Mr. Julius Simon given for American Red Cross workers and U.S. Army personnel. Henrietta, looking frail and petite, was photographed with a group of the guests. Mr. Frank Tweedy of the Red Cross held her arm for the photograph.

The refugee children continued to pour into Palestine. Twenty-one Turkish youths arrived at Haifa, and forty Yemenite boys and girls were scheduled to reach Suez. Vexations and baffling situations continued to plague Henrietta. "The Agudat business will drive me mad—eight little boys kidnapped in less than two weeks, and from a Mizrachi institution," Henrietta bewailed on November 20. "The Central authorities of the Agudat deny all complicity in the

---

* *(Philadelphia:* Jewish Publication Society, *1961),* 200.

deed, and avow that they can't trace the abductors.'' She was not worried about the children as she knew they were safe and under a roof and not starving. But the intensive conflict between Agudat Israel and Mizrachi over the placement of religious children had moved from the religious to the political field. She felt the squabbling had no elevating aspects.

As usual Henrietta was afraid of her approaching birthday with its widespread publicity. She was scheduled to speak in the morning at the annual meeting on December 21 of the Le-Maan Ha-Yeled Ve-Ha-Noar, the Fund for child and Youth Care. In the evening she was to speak again at the twenty-fifth anniversary of the Hadassah Nurses' Training School. In addition she would have to meet a transport of forty-six youths from Turkey. She was perplexed as to how she could interview and place that number so quickly since not a single religious place was available.

Henrietta's nephew Benjamin had been stationed with his unit in Egypt. She wrote to him in early 1944, asking whether Cairo had gripped him as it had her:

> I loved it and I hated it. It's exquisite and it's intolerable from the human-humane point of view. I made up my mind if I ever got another opportunity to visit Cairo I'd devote myself to the study of the mosques through the centuries. The oldest one there is a marvel and stands far above many of the later ones as an art monument.

I am still occupied with the reception of the jetsam and flotsam that manages to reach these shores from Greece, Turkey, Lisbon, Nairobi, and Poland via Budapest. The mixture of languages is bewildering, an illustration of the effectiveness of the Tower of Babel punishment.

In mid-February the tenth anniversary of the arrival of the first Youth Aliyah group was celebrated. Henrietta and Hans Beyth conducted a tour for some thirty journalists, showing them as many types of Youth Aliyah groups throughout the country as they could crowd in. There was also a press conference at Haifa. All the arrangements for the tour and a broadcasting session had been made by Mr. Beyth and Mr. Spector of the Keren Ha-Yesod, the financial institution of the World Zionist Organization and of the Jewish Agency for Palestine. Henrietta wrote on February 20:

> It was most successful—all the arrangements turned out perfectly, including the weather, with the result that Youth Aliyah has been

given more publicity than in all the ten years of its existence together. The journalists knew nothing, nothing at all, of the movement. I was amazed at their utter ignorance. It served a purpose. The necessity of seeing our work through their uninstructed eyes brought home to me anew the importance and achievements of the undertaking. Last night, on the actual anniversary day, we had a broadcasting performance. I think it was universally considered successful.

Indeed the celebration, the journalists' tour at the beginning of the week and the radio program at the end, had put Youth Aliyah on the map. "You should see our clipping book—it's voluminous," Henrietta commented.

On the evening of March 13, Boston University used two-way short-wave radio to confer on Henrietta an honorary degree of Doctor of Humanities. Dr. Daniel L. Marsh, president of the University, characterized Miss Szold thus: "... distinguished for social settlement work in America and in Palestine; scholar, classicist, journalist; Founder of Hadassah; accomplisher of unparalleled reclamation and rehabilitation work in Palestine; a mother in Israel—through organizing and directing the Youth Aliyah, the joyful mother of ten thousand motherless children; you have spent your years as a tale that is told, and the tale is one of a life devoted to the pursuit of the beautiful, the true, and the good; by reason of strength, the days of your years are four score years and more, yet is their strength labor and joy..." Bertha Levin accepted the honor on behalf of her far-away sister.

Henrietta was scheduled to reply to the citation at 3:30 A.M. Eastern Standard time. Her voice came over the radio:

Humbly I express my deep appreciation in these days of men's inhumanity to man, to bear the title of Doctor of Humanities. It is not a slight honor. You promise me privileges connected with the honor...Is it possible to add to the privilege to represent the thousands of parents whose children have been educated for intelligent democratic citizenship in the homeland of the Jewish renaissance, and the tens of thousands who look for the rescue of their tortured children...?

And President Franklin D. Roosevelt sent Henrietta the following message:

Hearty congratulations as you celebrate the tenth anniversary of the Youth Aliyah movement, of which you are the honored founder.

Since 1889 when you organized the first English and Americanization classes in your native Baltimore, you have devoted yourself to the best social and educational ideals, both here and in Palestine. Your direction of Youth Aliyah has been characteristic of the qualities that have won you such respect and affection...

The coming liberation of Europe will present us all with unparalleled problems. We must heal broken bodies, rebuild shattered lives and faith. I am sure that in this task Youth Aliyah with your guidance will take its place to the forefront, as in the past.

CHAPTER 12

JOURNEY'S END

Henrietta was experiencing respiratory problems, aggravated by the acerbic dispute between the Mizrachi and Agudat Israel people. And Jewish extremists were causing trouble. She wished she did not know what was taking place in Palestine instigated by insurrectionary elements. "In Jerusalem we are living under curfew regulations," she wrote on March 26, 1944. "I am told that the havoc wrought by the bombs in Jerusalem, in the heart of the city, is appalling. Private property has been ravaged for blocks. Madmen!" She had been scheduled to motor to Haifa next day to greet new arrivals from Turkey, but her physician, Dr. Kleeberg, prohibited the journey. A few days later she was put to bed in the Hadassah Hospital. "My trouble seems to be exhaustion traceable, in my opinion, to the tra-ra-ram that has been raised round about the religious question," she wrote on April 1. "Today Mr. Beyth goes to Haifa to meet a group of 50 children from Turkey; he will have to decide the religious status of each one of them, and that is my responsibility." Henrietta supposed that in a week's time Rabbi Berlin would launch another "mean" article against her in his Orthodox journal, *Hatzofeh.*

While Henrietta was in the hospital, Emma Ehrlich and Hans Beyth came to see her daily. They kept her in touch with the world in general and with Youth Aliyah in particular, yet she chafed under her enforced neglect of business. She attended Seder celebrated at the hospital but was allowed to stay only the first twenty minutes, then was rolled back to bed. By mid-May she was well enough to move into an apartment at the Hadassah Nurses' Training School. There she had a Hebrew and an English secretary come to her for dictation, and she was able to meet with members of her staff. By June she was going to the office in the

76

mornings and working at the Training School during the afternoon.

On June 4 Rome fell, and on the 6th the Allies landed in northern France. By August 15 they were in southern France. "I am very glad that Aunt Henrietta is able to hear the glorious war news of these days," Benjamin wrote to Jastrow on September 5. "She can see 'the red dawn of the day' and we hope she may be spared to lay her stone among the foundation stones of the new era of peace."

In September the Russian armies forced the capitulation of Finland and Bulgaria, and the Jewish Brigade, made up of Jewish military units in Palestine, was formed as part of the British Army. But Henrietta was back in the Hadassah Hospital. She wrote to Benjamin on September 22:

> I sit up outside of bed twice a day. I walk—just now I managed three hundred steps (notice "managed"—it's not easy)—and before returning to bed I walk again. I must confess that getting back to bed is like getting home after a tiring journey.
>
> I have begun to read the daily paper though only cursorily. It is true, there is exhileration in the air such as we have not known there five years. But the fighting situation is still cruel, and the end is not so clearly in sight as it seemed to be a few weeks ago. I should very much like to hear your views on the Jewish Brigade. It goes down in history as a landmark on our steep road to national existence of the accepted kind.

After a stay at the hospital of three and a half months, Henrietta was back at the Nurses' Training School. Norman Bentwich called on her in what was to be his last visit. She spoke animatedly of the new and increased burden Youth Aliyah would have to undertake at war's end. She insisted on the need for careful preparation.

During her illness the press and radio issued bulletins on her condition, and the hospital was overwhelmed with inquiries from concerned persons. The end came at 7:40 in the evening of February 13, 1945. Next morning's *Baltimore Sun* carried the news of the death of "the foremost Jewish woman of modern times."

Henrietta's passing left the Jewish community of Palestine with a sense of personal bereavement. Thousands filed past her bier at the Hadassah School of Nursing. And thousands of mourners from all over Palestine escorted her to her last resting place on the Mount of Olives. Old and young they came despite the inclement weather. Had she not been largely responsible for bringing to Palestine 13,000 children from countries of Nazi persecution? She had requested that no eulogy be pronounced. Instead a Youth Aliyah boy aged fifteen, one of her Teheran children, recited the *kaddish*.

A month later many American leaders paid tribute to Henrietta at a memorial service held in New York City's Carnegie Hall. A passage read from the Book of Job, the book for which her beloved father had written a commentary, aptly described her life:

> I delivered the poor who cried, and the fatherless who had none to help him. He who was about to perish, blessed me. I caused the widow's heart to sing for joy. Righteousness was my garment and justice my robe. I was eyes to the blind, feet to the lame, a father to those in need. I searched out the cause of those whom I did not know. I dared reach out to the fangs of the wicked and pluck the victims from his grasp...

Henrietta's devoted secretary, Emma Ehrlich, wrote to Bertha Levin on March 20, 1945:

> Henrietta thought of you and spoke of you always. Either "Bertha" or "Betsy" were often on her lips—"my Betsy," "my pink and white Betsy, that dear." No one ever had a more loving sister than you. On that dreadful Thursday, December 14, when the physicians sentenced us to but a few more hours of her presence, she kept murmuring, "Bertha, Bertha." And then she said to me slowly, painfully, word by word in gasps, "Tell Bertha I thought of her with my last breath." The crisis passed, rather subsided. She lived to suffer cruelly for almost nine more weeks.

On July 21, 1946, an impressive ceremony took place at the unveiling of Henrietta's tombstone. Her long-time friend, Mrs. Rose Jacobs spoke, as did Mr. Harry Sacher, her colleague on the Palaestine Executive. Sprigs of myrtle, the symbol of Hadassah, were ranged round the tombstone. Some years later the grave was desecrated and the tombstone removed by the Jordanians who built a road through the burial ground. On February 15, 1968, a marker was placed on the side of the road, at the nearest point to where Henrietta Szold had been laid to rest. Rabbi Rakovsky, the Hadassah chaplain, recited the prayer for the deceased, and Mrs. David de Sola Pool, former president of Hadassah, extolled her memory. The group of Hadassah women at the ceremony shed tears. Two young people placed flowers on the new grave site. After all, children had been Henrietta's concern for so many years.

Mrs. Rose G. Jacobs speaking at the unveiling ceremony of the tombstone of Henrietta Szold's grave on the Mount of Olives, July 21, 1946.

Mr. Harry Sachar, Miss Szold's colleague on the Palestine Executive, speaking at the unveiling of her tombstone, July 21, 1946.

פ"נ

הנרייטה סאלד
בת הרב בנימין

ת נ צ ב ה

Mrs. David de
Sola Pool
extols
memory of
Henrietta
Szold,
February 15,
1968.

Ceremony at unveiling of Miss Szold's tombstone, July 21, 1946.

Members of Hadassah and others at ceremony at Henrietta
Szold's new grave site on Mount of Olives, February 15, 1968.

Two young people
place flowers on
new grave site on
Mount of Olives,
February 15, 1968